About this book

The Pressure Cooker explores a hidden world, one that often remains in the shadows and whispers of the overlooked or forgotten.

This is a world where harm and destruction occur, but the culprits are not always criminals or strangers. Often, these acts are committed by ordinary people, our friends and loved ones.

In moments of frustration, embarrassment, or insecurity, they explode and lash out, like a tornado released from the storm.

Through psychological insight and practical guidance, the Pressure Cooker reveals how emotional pressure can drive individuals to attack those closest to them, and how victims can navigate the confusing, painful aftermath with clarity and resolve.

The authors hope this book will appeal to those who have suffered physical or emotional injury from misguided aggression, as well as readers interested in relationships, psychology and trauma healing.

The Pressure Cooker discusses aggression born from feelings of inadequacy and frustration, and suggests ways to mitigate the damage, improve attitudes, and encourage healthier reactions going forward.

THE PRESSURE COOKER

Transforming Frustration into Resilience

Written by T.Wall & S.Wall

First published by Pickles Publishing Limited 2026
Copyright © Pickles Publishing Limited, 2026

A CIP catalogue record for this book is available from the British Library.
ISBN: 978-1-0369-5026-2

"I did then what I knew how to do.
Now that I know better.
I do better"

Maya Arigelou

CONTENTS

PREFACE

Frustration is one of the most universal human experiences, yet one of the least understood. It creeps into our daily lives, at work, in our relationships, in moments of performance, competition, or simply in the quiet spaces where our expectations collide with reality. Though often dismissed as a fleeting irritation, frustration carries enormous psychological weight. Left to fester, it can build pressure beneath the surface until it erupts in ways that surprise us, harm others, and leave lasting emotional traces.

This book grew out of personal experience and observation. We became increasingly interested not only in the visible consequences of frustration, but in the quieter, invisible psychological processes that precede them. Why do moments of disappointment sometimes escalate into anger? Why do otherwise reasonable people occasionally react in ways that harm those closest to them? Psychology offers important insights into these questions. Research suggests that frustration often arises when internal expectations collide with external reality. When our identity, competence, or sense of worth feels threatened, emotional pressure can accumulate rapidly.

If that pressure is not recognised or managed, it may spill over into behaviour that damages both personal wellbeing and relationships. *Pressure Cooker* seeks to uncover the emotional roots of these triggers and to understand why frustration so often transforms into aggression. We want to find ways to reclaim control over these powerful emotional responses. Drawing on psychology, behavioural science and neuroscience, we explore how internal vulnerabilities and external pressures intertwine to produce moments of emotional overload.

Pressure Cooker

At its core, this book is about transformation. Together we will explore how these reactions can be understood and redirected. Frustration does not need to lead to destructive outcomes. With awareness and the right practices, it can become a signal for reflection, growth, and improved emotional resilience. Most discussions about aggression focus on the aftermath, what someone did, how they behaved, the consequences that followed. Rarely do we pause to examine the fragile, often unseen moments that precede those actions: the rising tension, the simmering self-doubt, the sting of perceived failure, the heat of embarrassment or the public pressure to perform.

We, the authors, are eager to create a shift in perspective. Instead of accepting aggression as an inevitable and sudden explosion, we delve into the multi-layered determinants of mental processes, self-identity and societal influences. In doing so, we reveal aggression not as a mysterious loss of control, but as an understandable, preventable response to an overload of emotional triggers. *Pressure Cooker* gives a voice to experiences many people feel but cannot articulate. It offers reassurance that frustration is normal while making clear the responsibility that each of us must recognise, interrupt, and redirect impulses that may be harmful to others or ourselves.

In a world where expectations are high, scrutiny is constant, and emotional literacy is often overlooked, *Pressure Cooker* provides a roadmap toward healthier reactions and stronger resilience. Whatever your role in life, in the end, we are all simply humans trying to navigate the daily pressures of modern life. We have written this book for anyone who has felt overwhelmed by their own reactions, puzzled by the behaviour of others, or caught in the crosscurrents of expectation, comparison, and performance. It is also for those who support others in similar situations and believe that emotional awareness is as essential as any technical skill.

The Genesis of Frustration:
Recognising Emotional Triggers

In this chapter we explore the origins of frustration, delve into the various emotional triggers that ignite aggressive responses, and seek to weave together the theoretical frameworks and social influences that cause us to feel frustrated and how that frustration can at times boil over into inappropriate and sometimes harmful reactions.

Introduction

Most aggressive acts do not begin with violence.

They begin with frustration.

A missed expectation.

A small failure.

A moment of embarrassment.

History and psychology both show that many destructive actions emerge not from calculated malice, but from emotional pressure that has been allowed to accumulate without being understood or controlled. Frustration is an emotion we all experience. It often begins with a gap between what we expect and what happens. When reality falls short, that gap creates emotional pressure that can influence our behaviour. Mild frustration can motivate positive change, but chronic or intense frustration may lead to dysfunctional behaviour, including aggression, with far-reaching, sometimes harmful, consequences.

1.1. Understanding Frustration
1.1.1 What Is Frustration?

Frustration is an emotional response felt when we perceive an obstacle to the attainment of a desired goal. This multifaceted emotion encompasses anger, disappointment, helplessness, and anxiety. Classic theories, such as Dollard et al.'s (1939) frustration–aggression hypothesis, suggest that frustration naturally leads to aggression if not managed appropriately. In addition, subsequent research has refined this view, recognising that while frustration may increase the likelihood of aggressive behaviour, the outcome depends on various moderating factors, including differences in our temperament, ability to cope, and the situation we find ourselves in.

1.1.2 Dual Nature

Frustration, on the one hand, can signal that a goal is unattainable in its current form and prompt us to modify our approach. Yet, if mismanaged, frustration may lead to impulsive and aggressive reactions. This underscores the importance of understanding the roots of our frustration and develop strategies to manage its potentially destructive outcomes.

Learning to manage frustration helps prevent emotional responses getting out of control, which will ultimately enhance both personal and social well-being.

1.2 Frustration in Action: The Skiing Lesson

Let's picture a skiing lesson. An expert skier is patiently teaching a beginner, while both of their partners watch from the sidelines.

What could possibly go wrong?

Plenty!

First, there's performance pressure. The novice is trying to stay upright on two slippery, rebellious planks while gravity argues enthusiastically.

Then comes social comparison.

The expert glides down the slope with the effortless control of a Winter Olympian, while the beginner resembles a shopping trolley with a broken wheel. The fact that it's suddenly become a spectator sport only makes matters worse. Soon the brain hits cognitive overload. Instructions, embarrassment, icy terrain, and wounded pride all pile up at once. Rational thinking quietly packs its bags and leaves.

Finally, frustration finds an outlet. Instead of blaming the laws of physics, or their own lack of skill on the slopes, the novice redirects their irritation and crashes straight into the expert's partner. Psychologists, (Dollard et al., 1939; Marcus-Newhall et al., 2000) called this displaced aggression: when the real source of frustration is not confronted, the nearest innocent bystander becomes the unfortunate substitute target.

This "on the slope" drama demonstrates how internal triggers, like ego, self-esteem and embarrassment combined with external pressures, like an audience, expectations and comparison, can combine to produce behaviour nobody planned, least of all the person doing it. The lesson?

Spot your frustration early, preferably before someone gets scissor-tackled on the slopes.

1.3 Getting Triggered

Frustration does not emerge in a vacuum. It is a product of a dynamic interplay between internal preconceptions and external circumstances. When we consider both aspects, we understand the causes of our frustration and how to manage it.

1.3.1 Internal Triggers
1.3.1.1 Personality and Temperament

Personality traits strongly influence how people experience frustration. Those, of us with high levels of neuroticism, for example, are more prone to experiencing detrimental emotions in response to setbacks. Traits such as impulsivity and low frustration tolerance have been linked with increased aggression in the face of obstacles (Johnson & Miller, 2021). These internal influences may cause a person to view difficulties as personal attacks, which can lead to a stronger emotional outburst.

1.3.1.2 Self-Concept

Another crucial internal factor is our own self-concept. When personal identity is closely tied to competence or performance, any hint of failure can be profoundly destabilising.

This discrepancy between expectation and actual performance creates a fertile ground for frustration. Someone who prides themselves on being an expert in a particular domain may experience intense frustration when faced with tasks that expose their vulnerabilities. Recent work by Lee et al. (2022) emphasises that the more central a domain is to one's self-identity, the more significant the emotional impact of perceived failure.

1.3.2 External Triggers
1.3.2.1 The Environment

External factors play a crucial role in igniting frustration. Environmental stressors, such as high-pressure social settings, competitive environments, and unpredictable circumstances, can exacerbate frustration. Pressure to meet external expectations can amplify our sensitivity to failure in front of others. This is evident in research conducted in performance-based fields, which finds that even minor errors under observation can trigger disproportionate emotional reactions.

1.3.2.2 Social Comparison

The social environment significantly shapes emotional responses. Social comparison theory (Festinger, 1954) explains that we tend to assess our social and personal value by comparing ourselves to others. When such comparisons highlight personal inadequacies, the resulting gap between self and others can lead to frustration and feelings of inferiority.

1.3.2.3 Role Expectations

Unclear or unmet role expectations can quickly trigger frustration, especially in close interpersonal settings. When expectations and reality diverge, emotional pressure builds.

Often the combination of difficulty, observation, and perceived judgment can intensify emotional distress. In such situations, frustration can escalate rapidly and may be redirected outward, often toward an unintended target.

Very much like the monkey that, after being bullied by a larger peer, seeks out and bullies a smaller monkey uninvolved in the original conflict. External pressures alone do not determine how individuals react. What matters equally is how those situations are interpreted.

1.4 The Cognitive Underpinnings of Emotional Triggers
1.4.1 Appraisal Processes

At the heart of understanding emotional triggers is cognitive appraisal, the process by which we, as humans, evaluate and interpret events. According to Lazarus' cognitive appraisal theory, emotions arise not solely from external events but from our subjective interpretation of those events.

Frustration is likely to emerge when a situation is seen as a threat or a challenge that exceeds one's coping aptitude. It has also been discovered that the way and speed at which we interpret a situation can influence whether frustration escalates into aggressive behaviour. Bottom line, two people can experience the same event but react very differently, depending on how they interpret it.

1.4.2 When Our Expectations are Violated

Frustration often begins when reality does not match what we expected. The greater the gap, the stronger the emotional response. A minor setback can feel significant if it clashes with a strong belief about how things "should" have gone.

This is particularly true in areas tied to identity or self-worth, where even small deviations can feel disproportionately important. As we'll see, this gap between expectation and reality is where frustration starts to take hold.

1.4.3 Self-Blame

The meaning we assign to a setback will shape how we respond to it. We can see it as a temporary challenge or a sign of personal failure. If we blame ourselves, we are more likely to feel frustrated, and self-doubt will grow, like a weed in an orchard, choking the promise of what could have been.

We will feel shame, insecurities will rocket, we will judge ourselves, perhaps a little too harshly and ultimately, we will sink into despair believing that we just don't measure up. Conversely, if we blame someone or something else for what goes wrong, it may, briefly, protect our self-esteem, but it does not resolve the problem.

Blaming others for our difficulties, especially if we feel that others are sabotaging us on purpose, rapidly turns our frustration into rage. Returning to the skiing lesson, the novice might first see his poor performance as proof that he's simply not good enough, which could lead to feelings of embarrassment and self-condemnation.

However, if that discomfort becomes too overwhelming, he may defensively start looking for someone or something else to blame.

If he then perceives, fairly or unfairly, that the situation has been caused by the teacher or even the teacher's partner, his frustration could explode into a retaliatory outburst. It has been proven that aggression is more likely when people reinterpret their setbacks as being caused by others rather than themselves.

Blame, whether aimed at ourselves or others, is not the answer. The path forward can only be found through understanding and behavioural change.

1.5 Inside the Frustrated Brain

To understand how frustration escalates, we need to look at how the brain responds under pressure. Emotional reactions are shaped by an interaction between two systems: one that responds quickly, and one that regulates that response.

When we encounter setbacks, perceived threats, or moments of embarrassment, the brain's emotional system reacts rapidly.

This response is automatic, generating feelings such as frustration, anger, or anxiety and preparing the body to act. Balancing this is the brain's regulatory system, responsible for impulse control, decision-making, and emotional restraint.

When functioning well, it allows us to pause, reassess, and respond rather than react. Nonetheless, this balance is fragile.

When we are under stress, sustained pressure or just plain tired, our self-control starts to slip and tempers rise.

Frustration builds fast and when it peaks, it can blow up into aggressive and inappropriate behaviour. At the same time, the body's stress response is activated.

Energy rises, perspective narrows, and the body gears into action mode.

In short bursts, this can be helpful, but if this situation lingers, it can work against us, making calm, measured responses harder to access as reactions become faster, more intense, and often disproportionate.

What matters is not just the reaction itself, but how early it begins. Understanding this process is important because it shows that emotional reactions are not simply a matter of willpower or self-control but also biology.

Conclusion

Frustration has a dual nature. It can motivate change but when left unmanaged, it can quickly lead to reactions that surprise us.

We have explored how frustration begins: the gap between expectation and reality, shaped by internal triggers, external pressures, and the way we interpret events. These elements combine to create emotional tension that, if left unchecked, can escalate.

What matters is not just the trigger, but how it is processed.

As we have seen, early signals often appear before the eruption, such as, subtle shifts in thinking including emotional and physical signals. Recognising these warning signs early creates an opportunity to consider an appropriate and moderated response.

The following chapters build on this foundation, explore how frustration unfolds under pressure and how it can be managed. When understood, frustration is not a problem to avoid, it becomes a signal for change.

-2-

When Frustration Fights Back
The Frustration-Aggression Hypothesis in Action

In simple terms: frustration loads the gun,
but the situation pulls the trigger.

Introduction

John Dollard et al, had an illumination in 1939, "when something stops us from getting what we want, we feel frustrated."

This is a very human concept and an emotion we have all felt more than once in our lives. Simples!

The problem arises in how that frustration is expressed. Left unmanaged, it can spill over into anger, confrontation, or even aggression. This became known as the Frustration–Aggression Hypothesis. Early theorists suggested a direct link:frustration leads to aggression. When a goal is within reach but suddenly denied, emotional pressure builds, and aggression was seen as the natural release.

Fortunately psychology, like us humans, evolved and Neal Miller later clarified that frustration does not inevitably lead to aggression. Leonard Berkowitz refined this argument even further, showing that frustration can create emotional tension, but whether or not that develops into aggression depends on the situation.

With this foundation in place, we now turn to how frustration intensifies under pressure, particularly during a "performance", where emotional demands are higher and nerves more vulnerable.

Performance demands not only technical proficiency but also considerable emotional resilience. When our self-worth is tightly bound to public evaluation, any sign of failure or perceived inadequacy can ignite a storm of emotional turbulence. Here, frustration is no longer a private experience, an internal state, but becomes instead an external force that drives us to "fight back".

That unsettled feeling can arise during any performance and the dynamics that contribute to its intensification are puzzling. As such, we will dig into the internal and external triggers that ramp up emotional responses and discuss practical strategies for mitigating adverse outcomes. We want to highlight the importance of having strategies both before and after any performance. We hope that these approaches will help you feel prepared and supported as you manage the emotions that accompany *"performance"* in whatever context they may arise. Our practical tips pull together insights from psychology to show how reshaping your thinking can help you to stay balanced through life's knocks.

2.1 The Performance
2.1.1 Under Observation

Whether you are a musician performing in a concert, an athlete taking part in a sports event or an employee sharing a new idea at work, performance anxiety can affect us all. Each of these moments is challenging because we are in the spotlight and prised open to judgment. The presence of an audience magnifies every action and mistake, leading to a phenomenon known as "evaluation apprehension," a state of heightened anxiety and fear of criticism that raises the emotional stakes. Simply being observed can alter cognitive processing and increase stress (Martinez et al., 2023). In these situations, people might see small setbacks as major failures, which can lead to disproportionate reactions.

When anticipation, expectations and anxiety combine, they can create a cycle where stress increases frustration, and that frustration further impairs our performance.

2.1.2 The Dual Role of Public Recognition

Performance can bring recognition, but it also comes with the risk of failure or being exposed. Many of us desire validation and this drives us to pursue excellence and "perform", but this double-edged sword also carries a fear of failing in front of others which, most of the time, gives us that extra push to do better, but sometimes this fear may lead to unintended consequences or performance paralysis. When people closely link their sense of self to how well they perform, falling short of expectations can feel like a threat to their worth, which conjures up feelings of humiliation and unrest.

This dual role of public recognition, as both a motivator and a potential source of distress, shapes how people feel during a performance, driving both their desire to succeed and their fear of failing. This is the unseen terrain where small mistakes turn into a major drama, and emotions explode onto centre stage.

2.2 Turbulent Waters
2.2.1 Emotional Turbulence

As we explored in chapter one, our reactions are shaped less by what happens and more by how we interpret it. When a situation feels like a threat to competence or identity, emotions can escalate quickly. Frustration, anxiety, and self-doubt can begin to reinforce one another and a small setback, especially under observation, can lead to a disproportionate and detrimental reaction. Recognising this pattern is the first step to breaking it.

2.2.2 Emotional Volatility

We are all wired differently and how we react depends very much on our biology, our self-image and the circumstances. Emotional reactions during performance are influenced by the brain's regulatory systems.

As outlined earlier, when the brain's emotional system overrides its regulatory control, reactions become faster, stronger, and harder to manage, especially when under pressure. If not managed effectively, it will become more difficult to regain control and respond constructively.

2.3. The Counterattack: When Emotions Fight Back
2.3.1 When the Mask Slips

When pressure and scrutiny come together, frustration rarely stays hidden and often surfaces as anger, withdrawal, or self-sabotage.

What should remain contained is amplified. Athletes may react with visible outbursts that disrupt performance and team dynamics.

In professional settings, a brief lapse can shift tone, derail communication, and damage credibility.

2.3.2 The Role of Self-Expectations

High personal expectations can lead to frustration. Ambitious goals may make unmet objectives seem like a huge personal failure.

This inner conflict occurs when expectations are not aligned with reality, and this in turn amplifies our frustration, for example, a musician recognised for consistently flawless performances may perceive a single missed note as a failure. This discrepancy between belief and outcome frequently results in feelings of irritation and shame.

Roberts and Allen (2023) found that when people believe the stakes are high, they tend to overreact more often, even to small changes from what was originally expected.

2.3.3 Failure and Its' Social Dynamics

Social comparison becomes especially powerful during performance. When people measure themselves against others, particularly in public settings with high visibility, perceived shortcomings can intensify feelings of inadequacy and lead to emotional volatility.

As Smith et al. (2023) noted, the interplay between personal failure and social evaluation is a potent trigger that can lead to both overt aggression and covert self-sabotage.

2.4 Strategies for Navigating Emotional Turbulence
2.4.1 Developing Emotional Awareness

The first step to navigating emotional swings is awareness. This means noticing the early signs of frustration or anxiety, whether physical, such as a racing heart or sweaty palms, or cognitive, such as spiralling thought loops.

Methods like journalling for mood tracking, and biofeedback devices, like smart watches, can help bring these symptoms into focus, making changes visible in real time allowing for earlier recognition.

2.4.2 Cognitive Restructuring and Reframing

Cognitive reframing techniques empower us to reinterpret setbacks as opportunities which allows us to grow. If instead, these setbacks were seen as failures our self-image could be adversely tarnished

In public settings, this might involve shifting focus from "I must be perfect" to "I will do my best, and one mistake does not define me." Research by Kim and Park (2020) demonstrates that when we stop putting ourselves down, we are less likely to experience a rapid escalation of frustration.

2.4.3 Mindfulness

Mindfulness is very effective in helping us to control our emotions under pressure. The techniques practiced, such as deep breathing, meditation, and progressive muscle relaxation, help us to activate the parasympathetic nervous system, which counteracts the fight-or-flight response. Athletes and performers can benefit from mindfulness exercises before stepping onto the stage or into the field. These practices enable them to stay in the moment, reducing the impact of intrusive thoughts and allowing for a more focused performance.

2.5 Performance and Emotional Turbulence
2.5.1 The Missed Step

Imagine a dancer known for precise, expressive performances. During a live show, she slightly mistimes a turn, barely noticeable to the audience, but immediately obvious to her. In that moment, a thought cuts in, leading to self-doubt and frustration, *"I've ruined the entire performance."* Her focus shifts inward, her muscles become tense, and the fluidity that once defined her performance begins to falter. As she becomes increasingly aware of the audience's gaze, each step feels heavier, and the performance loses its natural rhythm. In that moment, the dancer thinks, "Everyone will see me as a failure." This thought triggers a fast heartbeat and a rush of adrenaline, making the on-stage distress obvious to all.

This scenario shows how even a minor misstep, when magnified by being in the spotlight and having high expectations, can be disruptive. It highlights why it is important not only to prepare technically, but also mentally, before any performance.

2.5.2 The Athlete Under Pressure

In competitive sports, the stakes are equally high. An elite athlete, known for consistent performance, struggles during a critical match. As the pressure mounts and every move is scrutinised by a live audience and commentators, the athlete's internal narrative shifts to self-criticism. The mounting frustration triggers an impulsive outburst, a momentary lapse that affects his performance and ignites conflict with teammates and opposing players.

Athletes who experience intense performance pressure are more prone to display aggressive behaviour when their self-expectations are not met. This scenario exemplifies how high visibility, internalised pressure, and social comparison can lead to emotional turbulence that undermines performance and interpersonal relationships.

Coaches and sports psychologists are increasingly incorporating stress-management strategies into training regimens to address these challenges, thereby helping athletes channel their frustration constructively.

2.5.3 The Presentation Fiasco

In the corporate world, performance often appears in the form of a presentation. One executive tasked with pitching a new business strategy to key stakeholders confidently begins the presentation.

Nonetheless, when a difficult question from an influential board member catches him off guard, his carefully maintained composure falters. The unexpected challenge triggers a wave of anxiety and loss of confidence, resulting in a defensive tone and what ends up becoming a disjointed presentation. The executive's inability to navigate his emotional turbulence undermines the pitch.

This scenario shows how performance pressure, in this case giving a presentation, can quickly turn into anxiety and frustration when things don't go as planned. The executive's experience is a reminder that preparation isn't just about knowing the material; it's also about managing your emotions and having healthy coping strategies in place. Practising role-play and taking part in stress-management workshops can help professionals build the resilience they need to stay composed and handle unexpected challenges.

2.6 Managing Public Performance Anxiety
2.6.1 Pre-Performance Preparation

Effective management of emotional turbulence begins long before stepping into the public spotlight. Pre-performance preparation should involve not only technical rehearsals but also emotional conditioning.

Techniques such as visualisation, where performers imagine successfully navigating stressful scenarios, can build confidence and reduce anxiety. Incorporating relaxation exercises and meditation into a pre-performance routine can also help regulate physiological responses, laying the groundwork for a composed presentation.

2.6.2 In-the-Moment Strategies

Even with thorough preparation, unanticipated challenges may still arise during a performance.

Developing in-the-moment strategies is critical to mitigating the impact of sudden frustration. Simple techniques like slowing breathing, taking notice of the surroundings, and using calmer, more balanced self-talk can help steady emotions in the moment.

2.6.3 Post-Performance Reflection and Growth

After a performance, reflective practices are invaluable for processing the experience and extracting lessons for future improvement. Practices already recommended like journaling or debriefing with trusted colleagues can enable us to critically analyse our responses, identify patterns in emotional triggers, and develop strategies for better managing similar situations in the future. This reflective process can help to transform potentially harmful experiences into opportunities to learn and build resilience.

2.7. A Combined Approach
2.7.1 Best Strategies

The most effective strategies combine mindset and practice. When people learn to challenge unhelpful thoughts and then rehearse in real-life scenarios, like practice presentations, confidence builds and anxiety is lowered.In simple terms, these treatments help us to rethink the self-defeating thoughts that fuel our anxiety while also providing hands-on tools to manage emotions.

2.7.2 The Role of Technology

Digital apps are playing an increasingly prominent role in controlling emotional instability and turmoil. As we know, many apps offer guided meditation and mindfulness, like, Petit Bambou, Calm, Headspace, The Mindfulness App and Serenity, as well as many more.

Using meditation apps regularly can reduce stress, improve focus, and help us all get improved shut eye. Biofeedback apps are also helpful because they show us how to calm our minds while also giving factual evidence, in real time, about what's happening in our bodies, 59Breaths, Elite HRV Wellness, WellHero, HeartPeace and Muse are a few that could be helpful.

With practice and consistent use, we can build, step by step, improved stress resilience, self-control, and overall self-awareness. It's like having a window where we can look into our bodies and learn how to respond rather than react.

Daylio, like many other mood tracking apps, is also popular. A type of mood diary that lets you quickly log your daily emotions and activities with icons and short notes. It then turns your entries into easy-to-read charts and statistics so you can spot patterns in your emotional life over weeks and months, helping you to understand what situations impact your mood. This type of mood-tracking app helps us to recognise triggers, supporting self-reflection and showing how factors like sleep and stress affect our feelings.

This type of monitoring or documenting, when used consistently, can improve emotional self-regulation, reduce anxiety and mood swings. We can monitor our stress levels and plan proactive coping strategies throughout the day. Digital aids can be combined with traditional therapy, particularly for those of us with limited in-person support (Evans et al., 2023).

Combining the regular use of apps into our daily routine, as we do, or should do, with exercise, will help us to remain steady, manage waves of conflicting feelings and strengthen our confidence and resilience.

2.7.3 The Professionals

Entities now recognise the unique challenges of performance for their staff and have begun to implement specialised training focused on management of feelings and stress. These programmes are designed to equip professionals with a toolbox of techniques to help them maintain composure under pressure, ultimately transforming frustration from a debilitating force into a manageable and motivating factor.

2.8. The Interplay of Culture & Identity
2.8.1 Cultural Norms and Emotional Expression

Cultural factors significantly influence how we perceive and express frustration. In some cultures, open displays of emotion are discouraged, leading people to internalise stress and potentially experience more intense and tumultuous feelings.

In others, expressing emotions openly is valued as a sign of authenticity and passion. These cultural norms shape the strategies people use to cope with performance anxiety and frustration, for instance, certain cultures which emphasise collectivism, putting the needs of family and the community before one's own, may inadvertently suppress healthy expressions of frustration, resulting in fiery flare-ups when the pressure becomes unsustainable.

Understanding these cultural dimensions is crucial for developing tailored treatments that respect diversity and what is considered "normal" in different communities.

2.8.2 When Conformity is Mandatory

When we perform, our identity is intertwined with our perceived success. This is especially true in professions where success directly reflects our personal worth.

When a performance fails to meet personal and societal standards, the resulting cognitive dissonance can lead to an intense internal conflict. If we have a rigid or overly narrow sense of self-identity, we are particularly vulnerable to the adverse effects of public failure, but if we cultivate a more flexible and multifaceted self-perception, we can build a buffer against harsh criticism.

2.8.3 Performance Evolves

The rapid growth of social media has increased the stakes regarding performance. Live streaming, on-demand content and multiple social media platforms have expanded the audience for many forms of performance.

This has amplified both the opportunities and the risks that come with living in the public eye. When mistakes linger online indefinitely and content can spread in seconds, even a brief lapse in judgment or a moment of frustration can echo far beyond what we ever intended, often turning a fleeting moment of embarrassment into, what could become, a lifelong humiliation.

Will these modern dynamics influence our emotions uniquely, possibly in ways not previously seen, and how can we better manage the anxiety that evolves with it?

2.9. Turning Frustration into Fuel
2.9.1 Understanding Both Sides of Frustration

Sometimes, our frustration can be overwhelming, but if we manage our emotions correctly, these situations will create an opportunity for transformation. When handled well, the energy behind this intense

emotion can fuel determination and sharpen the mind. If we can understand the source of our emotional unrest, we can start to build stronger coping strategies and channel that frustration into concentration, rather than letting it undermine our performance.

2.9.2 Practical Roadmap for Performance

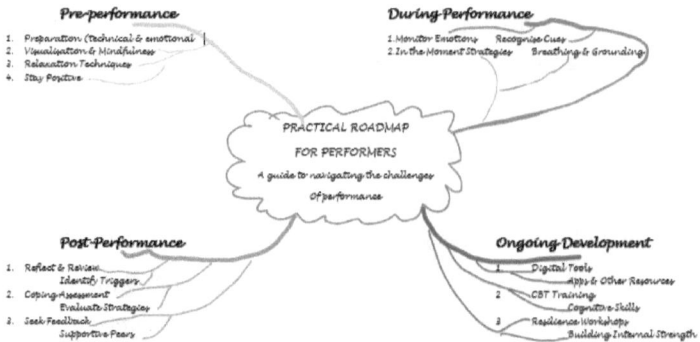

Conclusion

Performance is the albatross where personal identity, high expectations, and external judgment converge. When frustration shows its ugly face, it does so by tapping into deep-seated fears and vulnerabilities, often leading to uncontrolled outbursts, loss of temper or some form of emotional turbulence that can derail even the most prepared person.

There are multifaceted dynamics of performance anxiety, from the neurobiological mechanisms that fuel emotional responses to the cognitive and social factors that amplify perceived failures.

While the pressures of performance can be formidable, they also provide a unique opportunity for personal growth, if we can learn to navigate our emotional responses effectively by embracing emotional awareness and cognitive flexibility with a supportive network, we can transform frustration into a source of creative energy and resilience.

In an era where the boundaries between public and private are increasingly blurred, developing the skills to manage emotions is critical for our well-being.

As we continue to explore and refine these strategies, we hope that frustration will no longer be an uncontrollable adversary but a catalyst for growth, innovation, and sustained success.

-3-
When Self-Expectation Falls Short

Have you ever wondered why high personal standards and self-expectations backfire? We hope the following provides some insight into the ways self-expectations influence our feelings and, consequently, how we react.

Introduction

Each person carries an internal picture of who they believe they should be. These self-expectations can motivate growth and achievement. Nevertheless, when expectations become rigid or unrealistic, the gap between aspiration and reality can trigger frustration, shame, and self-doubt. As we saw earlier, frustration often starts with a gap between expectation and reality. Here, that gap becomes more personal, it's about who we think we should be not who we are.

This feeling of personal inability isn't just about lacking skill, it's often a mix of mindset, stress, expectations, and situation. Sometimes it's low confidence or fear; other times it's fatigue, pressure, or simply not having learned the skill yet.

Social comparison and unrealistic standards can make it worse, turning normal growing pains into self-doubt. In many cases, what feels like failure is part of development, not a permanent flaw, but a step on the ladder to improvement.

This phenomenon of personal inability, not being able to meet certain expectations or cope effectively with a situation will now be discussed from several different perspectives.

3.1 The Foundations of Self-Expectation
3.1.1 Self-Expectation and Personal Inability

Self-expectations develop through a process of internalisation in which external values, social standards, and personal experiences become part of our identity. These expectations act as benchmarks against which we measure success.

Personal inability emerges when performance falls short of these internal standards, creating a perceived gap between who we believe we should be and what we are able to achieve.

This gap can occur in our professional achievements, creative endeavours, or personal relationships and is sadly experienced as a failure if we are unable to live up to these internalised ideals. When we make a wrong move, it quickly spirals into harsh self-judgment, which rapidly leads to self-doubt and the occasional burst of misplaced aggression.

3.1.2 Just Perfect

Perfectionism often lies at the heart of unrealistic self-expectations. People with perfectionistic tendencies set excessively high standards and frequently interpret mistakes as evidence of failure. Rather than viewing errors as part of learning, perfectionists may treat them as a reflection of their own value.

3.1.3 Self-Expectation

Self-expectations are formed early in life through a variety of channels. Parenting styles, educational experiences, and peer interactions all contribute to developing the internal standards we each hold.

Children who receive praise only when they meet specific high standards may learn to equate their self-worth with high achievement and these early experiences can solidify into rigid internal benchmarks that continue to influence behaviour into adulthood.

3.2 How Inability Shapes Our Self-Perspective
3.2.1 Self-Perspective and Achievement

Self-perspective is the story we tell ourselves about who we are. When that story is glued to achievement, even a slight deviation can feel like a full-blown identity crisis. Particularly in high-pressure environments, what you do can start to feel like who you are, so even small mistakes feel personal.

3.2.2 Conflict and Blame

Cognitive dissonance arises when a conflict exists between self-expectations and actual performance. This inconsistency is a primary source of distress because it forces us to confront aspects of ourselves that we would rather not face. In many cases, this confrontation leads to blaming ourselves or self-blame, a process where we attribute our inability solely to personal shortcomings. Lazarus (1991) explains that the emotional response to cognitive misalignment can be so intense that it triggers defensive mechanisms such as anger, denial, or even self-sabotage.

3.2.3 The Impact on Self-Esteem

Self-esteem is often directly affected by personal inability. When we internalise failure, it can lead to a pervasive sense of inadequacy. Repeated experiences of falling short of one's expectations can erode self-esteem over time, making it increasingly difficult for us to bounce back from setbacks.

This diminished self-esteem, in turn, may contribute to a vicious cycle where lowered confidence further impairs performance, reinforcing the belief that we are fundamentally stupid.

3.2.4 How Others Reflect Our Inadequacies

Social comparison plays a significant role in shaping self-expectation. In situations where success is often sought, such as at work, sports, or in academia, we often gauge our abilities against the achievements of our peers.

When comparisons consistently underscore our shortcomings, our sense of incompetence is amplified. This "social mirror" intensifies feelings of worthlessness and compounds the emotional distress associated with unmet expectation. As Davis and Roberts (2021) note, the interplay between personal failure and social judgment can be particularly damaging.

3.3 What Underlies Personal Inability
3.3.1 The Role of Attributional Styles

As discussed earlier, attributional style refers to how we explain success and failure. When people attribute setbacks to fixed personal flaws rather than situational factors, feelings of inadequacy and frustration intensify.

3.3.2 Perfectly Overgeneralising

Perfectionists have a habit of turning one setback into a sweeping verdict. Fail one exam, and suddenly it's, *'I'm just not cut out for this.''* That kind of overgeneralising twists reality and hits harder than it should, fuelling stress and, over time, even leading to depression.

3.3.3 The Cycle of Rumination

Rumination, or the repetitive focus on distressing thoughts, is another psychological mechanism that can exacerbate feelings of inadequacy.

If we dwell on our shortcomings, we create a feedback loop of counterproductive reasoning which further diminishes our self-esteem and amplifies emotional distress.

Rumination, which is not to be confused with reflection, tends to keep us stuck. Reflection, on the other hand, encourages curiosity and is constructive. It helps us to learn, adjust, and grow.

Instead, rumination is repetitive and self-critical, replaying the same thoughts without offering a solution.

Reflection creates clarity; Rumination drains energy.

Rumination is a predecessor of lingering fatigue and loss of motivation. It impedes effective problem-solving and makes it more difficult to break free from a cycle of low self-regard.

3.4 The Biology of Not Feeling Good Enough
3.4.1 The Brain & Emotions

As discussed earlier, emotional reactions to perceived failure are shaped by the brain's regulatory systems. When stress overwhelms these systems, responses can become more intense and harder to control.

3.4.2 The Chemistry Behind Feelings

Your mood isn't just mindset, it's chemistry. Neurotransmitters like serotonin and dopamine help regulate how steady, motivated, and emotionally balanced you feel. When serotonin dips, irritability rises, impulses get louder, and low mood creeps in. When perfectionists fall short, stress ramps up, throwing things further off balance and making counterproductive thoughts harder to shake off.

The good news?

When those neurochemical imbalances are addressed, the emotional fallout from poor performance can ease. It's not always a character flaw, sometimes it's just brain chemistry under the strain of everyday life.

3.4.3 Hitting the Panic Button

When we feel that we have failed, the body does not remain calm. It starts to release cortisol and adrenaline, the chemical equivalent of a fire alarm.

Helpful? In real danger, absolutely!

Helpful during a presentation or a tough conversation? Not so much.

Too much cortisol can fog up thinking and weaken self-control. When stress becomes chronic, it creates a vicious loop: feelings of inadequacy, performance dips and stress increase. Understanding this biology matters because sometimes the problem isn't a lack of ability, it's a nervous system blocked in overdrive.

3.5 How Self-Expectation is Shaped
3.5.1 The Pressure of Societal Standards

We live in a culture that treats success like a personality trait. We begin our young lives with school report cards that in adulthood changes into LinkedIn updates framing our career successes.

The message is loud and clear: achieve more, be better, don't fall. Somewhere along the way, excellence stops being a goal and starts feeling like an obligation to prove our worth.

The problem? Those standards are sky-high and rarely sustainable.

When setbacks happen, and they always do, the gap between the gloss and real life can feel brutal. In a world that worships winning, it's easy to forget that being human, sometimes, includes losing too.

3.5.2 The Role of Social Media and Public Scrutiny

As noted earlier, the digital age has further exacerbated performance pressure. Social media platforms present carefully curated images of success and perfection while we compare our struggles with the perfect lives of others.

This skewed comparison intensifies low self-esteem and reinforces unrealistic expectations.

The constant feedback loop of likes, shares, and comments creates an external validation system that can distort self-worth and makes us feel even more exposed when we fail.

3.5.3 Family Dynamics and Early Experiences

Family expectations don't just shape behaviour; they shape the story we tell ourselves about our value. When love feels tied to achievement, even subtly, the message can land as "you're valued when you succeed." Gradually that can turn our self-worth into what feels like a performance review.

The trouble is, when approval feels conditional, confidence becomes fragile. One stumble doesn't just feel like a mistake, it feels like a verdict.

Children raised in high-pressure, high-expectation environments are more likely to grow into perfectionists, and more likely to unravel emotionally when things go wrong.

In short, when love feels earned, failure feels like having it taken away.

3.5.4 Culture

Academic and professional institutions often reinforce high standards and performance metrics. The pressure to excel can become overwhelming in competitive environments where success is measured by grades, awards, or promotions.

The resulting fear of failure can lead to dysfunctional coping strategies, such as procrastination, self-sabotage, or even avoidance of challenges altogether. Studies in educational psychology reveal that environments that do not encourage risk-taking or stigmatise failure tend to produce people who are less resilient and more prone to the adverse effects of unmet self-expectation.

3.6. Snapshots
3.6.1 The Academic Prodigy Who Lost Her Way

Consider the case of a high-achieving student who, from an early age, was celebrated for her academic prowess. As she progressed through school, the accolades and recognition became intertwined with her sense of identity. When she entered university, a setting that demanded even higher levels of performance, she began to struggle with the increasingly complex material. Despite her past successes, she found herself unable to maintain the same level of performance. Each setback was perceived not merely as a poor grade but as a personal failure that undermined her entire identity. As the years passed, her self-esteem plummeted, leading to severe anxiety and depression. This story illustrates how early internalisation of high self-expectations can result in catastrophic emotional consequences when reality falls short.

3.6.2 The Professional Under Pressure

The pressure to meet self-imposed benchmarks is equally intense in the corporate world. One executive, known for his innovative ideas and impeccable track record, began to experience a series of setbacks. A failed project, compounded by harsh feedback from peers and superiors, made him question his abilities.

The resulting sense of personal inability impaired his decision-making skills and strained his relationships with colleagues. Desperate to compensate, he began micromanaging his team, eroding trust and collaboration. This example underscores the cyclical nature of personal inability: unmet expectations lead to emotional distress, which undermines performance, creating a self-reinforcing loop of failure.

3.6.3 The Athlete's Battle with Self-Doubt

In competitive sports, the pressure to perform is often visceral. An elite athlete renowned for his speed and agility found himself grappling with a sudden decline in performance. Despite rigorous training and previous success, several minor mistakes eroded his confidence.

The athlete internalised each error as evidence of personal inadequacy, even though external factors, such as changes in training routines and increased competition, also played a role. His inability to cope with these setbacks led to increased frustration and a deterioration of his on-field performance.

This scenario highlights how self-expectation and personal inability can have immediate and tangible effects on performance and why targeted treatments are crucial for athletes vulnerable to such psychological pitfalls.

3.7 Learning How to Cope
3.7.1 Cognitive-Behavioural Approaches

As discussed earlier, cognitive behavioural approaches focus on how our interpretations shape emotional responses. Techniques such as cognitive restructuring help individuals identify and challenge self-defeating thinking patterns, replacing them with more balanced and realistic perspectives.

When perceived failures or limitations are reframed, harsh self-judgement can be reduced allowing for challenges to be tackled with greater clarity and control. Over time, a poor performance can be remembered as an isolated incident rather than a pervasive personal flaw.

3.7.2 Cultivating Self-Compassion

Self-compassion is a critical component in mitigating the adverse effects of unmet self-expectations. Rather than harshly criticising ourselves for perceived failures, we are encouraged to adopt a kinder, more understanding stance toward our shortcomings. Taking actions like acknowledging one's pain without judgment, recognising that imperfection is part of the human experience and maintaining a mindful awareness of one's feelings has been associated with lower levels of anxiety and frustration, acting as a buffer against the harmful effects of feeling inadequate.

3.7.3 Mindfulness and Stress Reduction

Mindfulness-based stress reduction (MBSR) techniques can help us become more aware of our internal experiences without becoming overwhelmed. If we practise mindfulness, meditation and deep-breathing exercises, or even yoga, we can learn to observe our self-defeating thoughts and feelings as transient mental events rather than reflections of a permanent reality. This shift in perspective can significantly reduce the emotional intensity associated with perceived limitations.

3.7.4 Building Resilience Through Social Support

As mentioned earlier, supportive relationships play an important role in regulating emotional responses. Family, friends, and mentors can provide perspective, reassurance, and practical guidance during difficult moments. These connections help reduce emotional intensity and challenge distorted reasoning, making it easier to respond constructively.

3.7.5 The Future of Personal Growth

As society increasingly values resilience and adaptability, the way that self-expectation is understood is also evolving. Already there is a push to balance the drive for excellence with the need for self-care. If we combine the insights from psychology, neuroscience, and cultural studies, it may be possible to develop strategies that empower people to pursue goals without sacrificing emotional well-being.

Conclusion

Understanding feelings of inadequacy rooted in high self-expectation is both challenging and transformative. This chapter has explored how the gap between who we aspire to be and who we are can trigger intense emotional reactions, leading to cycles of self-doubt, frustration, and, in some cases, aggressive behaviour. Examining the interplay of cognitive, neurobiological, and social factors gives us a nuanced perspective on why self-expectations can sometimes become a double-edged sword.

Far from being an immutable flaw, the experience of failure offers a unique opportunity for growth. When we learn to recalibrate our internal standards and cultivate self-compassion, we can break free from the cycle of chronic self-criticism and emotional distress.

When we embrace imperfection and understand that setbacks are opportunities for learning, it is possible to transform the pain of unmet expectations into a source of motivation.

In the end, overcoming any failure is not about resigning oneself to mediocrity but about creating a more compassionate and realistic self.

Pressure Cooker

It is possible to strive for excellence without demanding perfection, humans aren't robots, we come with built-in glitches.

Let's acknowledge our limitations and learn to work with them rather than against them.

Only in this way can we open the door to a richer, more authentic experience of personal achievement, one that is defined not solely by success but by growth, adaptability, resilience and the courage to look our vulnerabilities in the eye.

-4-

Under the Spotlight

Introduction

Performance is a ubiquitous aspect of modern life. Whether you are an artist, an athlete, or a professional, we are continually called upon to perform under the watchful eyes of others. In such settings, the pressure of social evaluation can both enhance performance by motivating excellence and undermine it by triggering intense anxiety and self-doubt. Social pressure, the power of not only meeting one's own expectations but also the anticipated expectations of others, can create internal suffering. In the end, performance in public settings is inevitably shaped by social scrutiny; whether its effects are constructive or destructive depends on how the situation is managed.

4.1 The Nature of Performance
4.1.1 Defining Performance

Performance, in its broadest sense, refers to any activity or behaviour that is subject to observation by an audience. In performance arts, this may include concerts, theatrical plays, or dance recitals; in sports, it means competing before spectators and media; and in the corporate world, it is represented by performance targets, presentations, pitches, and live demonstrations.

What links these diverse environments is that each person's individual actions are transformed into a spectacle, a process where performance is not only measured against objective criteria, like a technical skill, but is also evaluated through subjective lenses such as charisma and confidence.

It has been long noted that when individuals perform publicly, their behaviour is influenced not only by intrinsic motivational factors but also by the awareness of being observed and judged by others (Martinez et al., 2023). This combination of self-imposed standards and external expectations creates a "catch-22" that forces "performers" to constantly balance authenticity with a desire to meet perceived ideals.

4.1.2 The Psychological Impact of Being Observed

As we noted earlier, the moment others start watching, stress spikes, and even tiny mistakes steal the show. Tunnel vision sets in, self-awareness heightens to the point where every breath feels loud, every second seems to take an eternity and what would usually go unnoticed is thrust onto centre stage.

4.1.3 The Dual-Edged Sword of Performance

Performance can be both a source of motivation and a major source of stress.

On the one hand, the presence of an audience can elevate our energy levels, drive us to achieve higher standards, and create a sense of collective purpose.

On the other, the same social spotlight may activate deep-seated fears of inadequacy and trigger a cascade of intense feeling.

Literature suggests that the outcome of a performance is determined by the delicate balance between resilience, experience, and the nature of the circumstances (Davis & Roberts, 2021).

This dual nature of performance means that for some of us, the spotlight serves as an incentive to excel, while for others it fuels a nightmare of ongoing anxiety and self-doubt.

4.2 Social Pressure and the Dynamics of Evaluation
4.2.1 The Weight of Social Pressure

Social pressure kicks in when the expectations you hold about your life, your accomplishments and your social status start being compared with everyone else's progress. Suddenly you're trying to keep up with the Joneses!

We're all familiar with the need to tick the right boxes, in other words meet certain standards, if you want to fit in, gain approval or earn admiration. Social pressure is often rooted in culture, media, and the expectations of significant others such as family, friends, and colleagues. In settings where success is publicly celebrated, this pressure is amplified by the constant bombardment of images and narratives that idealise perfection. As noted by Smith et al. (2023), the modern media setting often presents a distorted view of reality, one in which only success is visible, and failure is hidden behind a facade of perfection. This creates unrealistic benchmarks for achievement, intensifying the pressure felt by us, mere humans.

4.2.2 Mechanisms of Social Comparison

As we now know, when trying to understand performance dynamics, social comparison theory, proposed by Festinger in the 1950s, remains highly relevant even today. We naturally assess our abilities and achievements by comparing ourselves to others. When performing in public these comparisons become more salient because the audience itself can be a source of feedback and measurement.

In highly competitive settings, for example, teammates' exceptional performance can operate as a dual force, driving improvement while also sharpening awareness of one's own limitations.

The resulting disparity between one's self-assessment and the perceived benchmark can generate significant emotional strain. Davis & Roberts (2021) demonstrated that frequent social comparisons are often correlated with increased levels of stress, anxiety, and depression.

4.2.3 The Role of Anticipated Judgment

Anticipated judgment is the cognitive process whereby we imagine how we will be evaluated by others before, during, and after a performance.

This anticipation can modify behaviour in profound ways. Performers, for instance, may engage in "safety behaviours" such as rehearsing excessively or altering their natural style to conform to perceived audience expectations.

While these behaviours may be intended to minimise the risk of receiving harsh criticism, they can sometimes interfere with authentic performance and undermine the end result.

Anticipated judgment also affects physiological responses. Empirical evidence from brain scans has revealed that the mere thought of being scrutinised can activate areas of the brain associated with fear and anxiety, leading to an increase in stress hormones like cortisol. Suddenly your brain goes a bit offline, your memory checks out, and your performance falls well short of what you know you can do! Thus, the burden of anticipated judgment is both psychological and biological.

4.3 The Underpinnings of the Socially Charged Performance
4.3.1 Cognitive Appraisal and Emotional Regulation

As touched on in chapter one, how you read a situation, shapes how you feel about it. Treat a performance like a threat to your identity, and suddenly anxiety, frustration, and shame hits you in the chest. For many performers, constantly measuring themselves against sky-high standards warps their judgment.

One tiny mistake becomes "I'm a complete disaster," and the emotional fallout lingers long after the curtain falls. Classic catastrophising and overgeneralising is great for drama but terrible for performance anxiety.

4.3.2 Stress Hormones in Action

As we now know, in situations of heightened social evaluation, the body's stress response is activated, leading to a release of hormones. This release provides a boost in energy and concentration, but only temporarily.

Long-term, high stress hormone levels distort reasoning and emotional control. Elevated cortisol levels have been linked to diminished memory, reduced impulse control, and a general impairment of executive brain functions (Harris et al., 2021).

The cyclical nature of stress hormone release can be particularly damaging for performers. The anticipation of unforgiving judgement may trigger a pre-performance surge of cortisol, which then compromises the quality of the performance.
The resulting failure, in turn, elevates stress responses in the future, creating a self-defeating cycle that can lead to chronic performance anxiety and a shaken belief in competence.

4.4 Who Gets to Define Success?
4.4.1 How Culture Scripts Performance

The way society and culture define success and failure plays a central role in shaping our performance experience. Cultural stories, embedded in media portrayals and collective dialogue, often idealise perfection and present success as both attainable and obligatory. These narratives are reinforced through awards, accolades, and public endorsements, leading us to internalise a binary view of performance: one is either a winner or a loser. This dichotomy is internalised early in life, leading adolescents and adults to magnify even minor failures and experience imperfection as both a personal and public humiliation.

4.4.2 Group Dynamics & Peer Judgement

Beyond the broad impact of media and cultural narratives, the immediate social context of performance, such as peer groups, teams, and colleagues, exerts a powerful influence on us. In settings where success is collectively defined, the evaluation of one's performance is intertwined with group dynamics. Peer evaluation can be a double-edged sword: while supportive feedback can enhance self-confidence, unfavourable comparisons and criticism can increase low self-esteem.

Group dynamics often dictate that we conform to collective standards of excellence. Davis & Roberts (2021) revealed that environments characterised by competitive internal cultures can foster both high achievement and intense conflict. In such settings, the pressure to perform is compounded by the fear of letting the team down, leading to increased anxiety and self-monitoring, for instance, in team sports or work environments, our performance is not solely a personal matter, it reflects the group's collective identity.

4.5. Snapshots: Performance Under Social Pressure
4.5.1 The Musician Facing a Critical Audience

Imagine a renowned classical pianist preparing for a major international competition. In the weeks leading up to the event, the pianist is not only haunted by the fear of making a mistake in front of an astute and knowledgeable audience but also faces relentless media scrutiny and critical reviews from esteemed experts. In this scenario, every note played is subject to intense evaluation, and even a slight deviation from perfection may be judged harshly. The pianist experiences a mix of anticipation and dread, knowing that the outcome of the performance could define his career.

This example illustrates how the intersection of personal ambition and public expectation can create a pressure cooker situation. Research has shown that performers in such high-stakes situations often report feelings of heightened self-consciousness and anxiety, which can interfere with the flow of performance and lead to diminished creativity (Martinez et al., 2023).

4.5.2 The Athlete: When the Game Demands More

In competitive sports, the spotlight is often the harshest. Consider an elite track athlete who has consistently broken records and become a national hero. At a major international event, however, the weight of national expectation and media attention begins to overshadow the athlete's usual confidence.

As competitors push the boundaries of performance, the athlete finds that every stride is accompanied by an acute awareness of the public's gaze. An unexpected stumble or a momentary lapse in concentration is broadcast instantaneously, critiqued by commentators and dissected by millions on social media.

This scenario serves to highlight the vulnerability that even the most accomplished performers face under social pressure. The athlete's experience is emblematic of the broader issue that high public visibility can convert minor setbacks into public spectacles of failure.

The psychological impact of such public scrutiny has been linked to both acute performance anxiety and longer-term issues such as burnout and a sense of hopelessness.

4.5.3 In the Hot Seat

In the corporate world, how you "perform" is a different game, one that involves negotiation, public speaking, persuasion, management appraisals and the challenges of the boardroom. Imagine this scenario, a senior executive is scheduled to pitch a new strategic initiative to a panel of influential investors.

In the moments preceding the presentation, the executive grapples with an internal battle between the desire to exhibit confidence and the fear of exposing vulnerability. During the presentation, every question and critique from the board is magnified, and the executive's performance is relentlessly scrutinised for signs of weakness. Here, the social pressure is not only rooted in individual self-expectation but is also accentuated by the collective judgment of a powerful group. The dynamics in such settings are complex, the executive must navigate personal anxiety while managing the expectations of a diverse audience, often with competing interests.

This interplay of internal and external pressures can lead to a phenomenon known as "paralysis by analysis," where overthinking inhibits spontaneity and creativity.

Such experiences underscore the multifaceted nature of social pressure during a performance.

4.6. How to Manage the Social Spotlight
4.6.1 Prepared Beats Talented

One of the most effective ways to mitigate the stress of public performance is thorough pre-performance preparation.

This involves not only rigorous practice of the technical aspects but also mental rehearsal techniques such as visualisation. By imagining success and rehearsing the performance in one's mind, you can reduce anticipatory anxiety.

Visualisation practices allow you to build neural pathways similar to those activated during actual performance, thereby reinforcing confidence and familiarity with the task at hand.

4.6.2 You Don't Win Alone

Social support is a critical buffer against the adverse effects of public scrutiny.

Whether through formal mentoring programmes, peer support groups, or informal networks of friends and family, having a reliable support system can provide both emotional reassurance and practical advice.

Sharing experiences with others who have navigated similar challenges helps normalise the emotional turbulence of being in the spotlight and can inspire adaptive coping strategies.

4.6.3 Grow or Get Left Behind

Adopting a growth mindset, the belief that abilities and intelligence can be developed through dedication and hard work, is another powerful strategy for mitigating the weight of expectations.

When performers view challenges as opportunities for learning rather than as definitive judgments of their worth, as Eileen Gu mentioned in her interview after winning a gold medal in the recent Winter Olympics, they are less likely to be overwhelmed by fear of failure.

This mindset allows errors to be seen as a natural part of the learning process, allowing a rapid recovery and stronger emotional balance. A growth mindset is associated with greater resilience, higher motivation, and improved performance.

4.6.4 The Digital Edge

With digital tech now part of our everyday life, it's easier than ever to manage, so called, stage fright. Simple apps that offer guided meditation and real-time stress tracking help to support maintaining a calm and focused mind before and during those moments when all eyes are on us! When used alongside more traditional approaches, these apps can make it much easier to manage the impact of those irritable nerves.

4.7 Performance Without Burnout
4.7.1 Addressing Chronic Performance Anxiety

For some of us, anxiety around "being on display" can become an ongoing problem, affecting not just career success but our overall well-being.

Constant judgement and criticism, perceived or real, can keep our stress levels high over time, increasing the risk of burnout, depression, and even damage to our physical well-being. That's why supporting mental and physical health shouldn't be limited to moments of crisis, it needs to be part of our daily routine.

4.7.2 Fix the System, Not the Person

Fear of judgement and scrutiny is not solely a challenge for us as individuals; it is also shaped by the organisational and cultural settings within which we work and live. Offices, schools, universities and sports clubs all have a role to play in creating environments that support a healthy attitude to performance. Consider entities that promote a culture of constructive feedback rather than punitive criticism to help lower the incidence of performance anxiety. Initiatives such as resilience training programmes, stress management workshops, and teaching a collaborative work mentality have been shown to mitigate the downside of being in the spotlight. When we foster an atmosphere of shared learning and mutual support, these entities can help us to perform at our best without compromising mental and physical health.

4.8 Master of the Moment
4.8.1 Own Your Identity

Central to managing social pressure when "performing" is the ability to distinguish between external evaluations and intrinsic worth.
We know that any performance inherently involves judgment from others, but we, as individuals, also have the capacity to develop a resilient internal identity that is not solely defined by success or failure. If we can cultivate a sense of self that is anchored in personal values and continuous growth, we can navigate the spotlight, and the judgement of others, with greater confidence and less fragility.

4.8.2 Resilience in Motion

When we step into the spotlight, success isn't just about talent or skill, it is about our emotional resilience. The expectations of others will always change, and social media platforms will continue to reshape how we perform in public. It is vital that we are mentally strong and able to adapt. In order to be so, we must be proactive, open-minded and willing to try a well-rounded approach to handling pressure, which in the long-term will help us to be increasingly more confident.

Conclusion

Performance under social scrutiny is an arena marked by both extraordinary potential and profound vulnerability. We have now covered how the pressures of social evaluation, from anticipated judgment and cultural narratives to social media and peer comparisons, combine to create an environment that challenges even the most adept performers. The cognitive, neurobiological, and social mechanisms discussed have revealed that the stress of performance is not a transient phenomenon but one that can have a lasting impact on mental health and professional ability.

However, we have also provided a glimmer of hope.

Strategies rooted in cognitive-behavioural techniques, mindfulness and social support, demonstrate that with the right methods and mindset, we can transform social pressure from a paralysing force into a catalyst for growth.

If we integrate adaptive coping mechanisms and cultivate an inner identity that values progress over perfection, we can learn to harness the energy of the spotlight rather than be overwhelmed by it.

As Eileen Gu says, "I just try to learn something from every competition and keep pushing myself. I just want to keep pushing the sport and be the best version of myself."

This reflects her broader mindset of treating events not only as outcomes to win but as opportunities for growth and progress and is an example of how she manages external expectations that frame performance in strict win–loss terms.

At the end of the day, the path to success lies in understanding and managing the complex dynamics of public scrutiny and judgement. As we continue to improve our knowledge, we need to consider how to create more environments within our communities that celebrate both excellence and resilience.

-5-

Stress: The Hidden Toll

Introduction

In our fast-paced, performance-driven society, stress is an ever-present companion. While moderate stress can motivate and sharpen our focus, extreme or prolonged stress, what we term "emotional overload", can overwhelm the body and mind. Emotional overload happens when the body's stress response stays switched on for too long, affecting both how we feel and how we function.

Now we have reached the moment to delve into the mechanisms of how stress manifests in our body, the biochemical pathways involved, and the wide-ranging consequences of chronic stress on our health and behaviour.

We will explore classic stress theories, discuss the neurobiology of stress, including the role of the hypothalamic-pituitary-adrenal (HPA) axis and provide examples to illustrate how emotional overload impacts daily function. Our aim is to explain how stress affects the body and mind, why long-term emotional overload can lead to health problems, and what can be done to reduce stress and build resilience.

5.1 Understanding Stress: An Overview
5.1.1 Breaking Point

Stress often operates quietly in the background, gradually raising the pressure. When demand exceeds our ability to cope, frustration sprouts and our erraticism unravels.

At its core, emotional overload is when multiple stressors accumulate, exhausting our ability to cope and undermining our health. Stress can be acute (short-lived) or chronic (persistent). Whereas acute stress may trigger an adaptive "fight-or-flight" response, chronic stress contributes to long-term dysregulation of our body's systems. Primarily we will focus on chronic stress, which is a major contributor to debilitating conditions like, hypertension, depression, and weakened immunity.

5.1.2 Survival Mode vs. Burnout

From an evolutionary standpoint, stress should be adaptive. The fight-or-flight response provided early humans with the necessary tools to survive immediate physical threats. However, contemporary stressors, such as work deadlines, social pressures, and financial instability, tend to be psychological and persistent in nature. This misalignment means that while our bodies are still primed for acute emergencies, they are not well-suited to prolonged exposure to stressors, leading to wear and tear on the body, a concept sometimes referred to as allostatic overload. If allostatic overload occurs, the body's stress response systems are activated too frequently, and often, for too long.

When this happens, the sympathetic nervous system and the Hypothalamic–Pituitary–Adrenal Axis (HPA) axis, which is the body's central stress-response system and responsible for regulating stress hormones like cortisol are eternally activated. Stress becomes chronic rather than adaptive and the resulting physiological strain is detrimental to both health and performance. Allostasis is the process by which the body achieves stability through change. When the adaptive stress response is engaged repeatedly, allostatic load accumulates, ultimately resulting in the onset of illness.

5.1.3 Neurotransmitters & Neuroplasticity

In addition to hormones, stress alters neurotransmitter dynamics and affects neuroplasticity. Chronic stress often leads to reduced levels of serotonin, a neurotransmitter crucial for mood regulation and alterations in dopamine pathways involved in reward processing. Such neurochemical changes are associated with depression and anxiety.

Furthermore, stress can impact brain regions critical for memory and decision-making such as the hippocampus and prefrontal cortex (PFC). In addition, when cortisol levels are high, key brain regions are damaged, the growth of new neurons in the hippocampus is impaired and neural connections shrink in the prefrontal cortex.

5.2. The Physical Cost of Stress
5.2.1 When the Heart Takes a Hit

As discussed earlier, stress activates the body's fight-or-flight response, releasing hormones such as cortisol and adrenaline. While useful in short bursts, prolonged activation can impair emotional regulation and decision-making. Chronic stress is one of the most significant contributors to cardiovascular disease. Elevated cortisol and catecholamines increase heart rate and blood pressure, creating an environment conducive to atherosclerosis.

Over time, persistent high blood pressure damages blood vessel walls, accelerating plaque formation and elevating the risk for a heart attack or stroke.

Medical research has consistently linked high work-related stress with an increased risk of coronary heart disease. Part of this is driven by the body's stress systems, the HPA axis and the SAM response, which keep the body in a prolonged fight-or-flight state. Over time, this contributes to sustained hypertension.

5.2.2 When Immunity Falters

Another critical consequence of emotional overload is its impact on the immune system. Cortisol's immunosuppressive effects are well documented. Under chronic stress, the body's ability to fight off infections diminishes, and the inflammatory response can become dysregulated. Prolonged stress is associated with increased susceptibility to viral infections, slower wound healing, and an elevated risk of autoimmune conditions.

5.2.3 Hormones Go Haywire

Chronic stress has significant metabolic implications. Persistently elevated cortisol levels contribute to insulin resistance, which is a precursor to type 2 diabetes. Stress-induced alterations in metabolism may lead to changes in appetite, particularly an increase in cravings for high-sugar and high-fat foods, thereby promoting obesity.

The fat which is then stored around the midsection does not remain passive, it disrupts how the body uses sugar, increasing the risk of health problems and issues with blood sugar, weight, and heart health. Beyond glucose metabolism, stress disrupts the endocrine balance by interfering with reproductive hormones, often leading to irregular menstrual cycles in women and lowered testosterone levels in men. These hormonal imbalances do not just affect fertility but also quality of life.

5.2.4 The Mental Toll of Stress

Emotional overload not only wreaks havoc on the body but also exerts significant effects on the brain.

Chronic stress has been associated with memory deficits, impaired concentration, and reduced cognitive flexibility.

The neurotoxic effects of cortisol on the hippocampus can lead to difficulties in forming new memories and retrieving old ones. From a psychological perspective, when we are under constant stress, we are at higher risk for developing anxiety, depression, and burnout.

The continual activation of the stress response can alter mood regulation, leading to feelings of helplessness and chronic fatigue. These consequences are not only detrimental to our well-being but can also impair social interactions and workplace productivity.

5.3 The Vicious Cycle
5.3.1 Feedback Loops

One of the hallmark features of emotional overload is its tendency to create vicious feedback loops.

When stress becomes chronic, the very physiological changes it induces, such as elevated cortisol, impaired cognitive functioning, and poor sleep quality, can act as additional stressors.

This creates a self-perpetuating cycle where physiological impairments exacerbate emotional overload, which in turn further disrupts bodily systems.

Consider those sleepless nights when we are undergoing a particularly stressful period in our lives. Chronic sleep deprivation, often a consequence of stress-induced hyperarousal, can impair cortisol regulation. The result is a feedback loop where disrupted sleep leads to higher stress, and higher stress further impairs sleep.

5.3.2 The Ripple Effect

Feeling emotionally overloaded can affect the body and push us into habits that pile on even more stress. Unfortunately, in attempting to manage chronic stress, we tend to depend on unhealthy coping strategies, such as substance abuse, overeating, and social withdrawal.

These behaviours may provide short-term relief but unfortunately, they also contribute to long-term health problems.

Consider some-one who, in response to work-related stress, turns to alcohol to unwind. While alcohol may temporarily dampen the stress response, chronic consumption contributes to liver damage, disrupts sleep, and eventually worsens stress and anxiety.

These counterproductive coping behaviours create additional burdens on the body and mind, making it even harder to break free from the cycle of emotional overload.

5.4 Snapshots
5.4.1 The High-Pressure Executive

In many fast-paced corporate environments, executives are frequently exposed to prolonged emotional overload. Consider a senior manager in a multinational company who faced constant high-pressure deadlines and intense scrutiny from both peers and superiors.

Over time, she began to experience frequent headaches, sleep disturbances, and elevated blood pressure. Despite her high performance at work, she reported feeling constantly tired, anxious, and irritable. Her situation was emblematic of the adverse cardiovascular, metabolic, and psychological consequences of chronic stress exposure.

Treatment included structured stress management workshops, cognitive-behavioural therapy (CBT), and mindfulness training which eventually helped her to lower her stress levels and improve her health.

5.4.2 The Overburdened Student

University students often contend with intense academic pressures that can lead to emotional overload. Imagine a group of students preparing for final exams while juggling part-time jobs and other responsibilities.

Many reported chronic anxiety, difficulties with concentration, and pervasive feelings of inadequacy. Brain scans conducted on several students have identified reduced activity in the prefrontal cortex and shrinkage of the hippocampus associated with prolonged stress exposure, further underlining the potential biological impact of academic pressure for some students.

5.4.3 Professional Athletes and the Price of Perfection

Athletes in high-performance sports are another group vulnerable to emotional overload. Elite competitors subject themselves to rigorous training regimens and constant scrutiny. One notable example is a professional marathon runner whose chronic stress from intense competition resulted in recurring injuries, weakened immune response and diminishing performance.

Investigations into his condition revealed persistently high cortisol levels and signs of burnout. A combined treatment of physical recovery protocols with psychological counselling were required to help the athlete restore a balance between physical strain and mental resilience. This illustrates how a combined approach to managing stress can support recovery and build resilience.

5.5 Mitigating Emotional Overload
5.5.1 Mindfulness and Meditation

Mindfulness meditation has emerged as one of the most promising strategies for reducing the physiological consequences of stress. The mind is trained to remain present and non-judgmental; mindfulness helps to temper the overactivation of the HPA axis and can reduce cortisol levels, improve heart rate variability and enhance overall emotional regulation.

5.5.2 Cognitive Behavioural Therapy (CBT)

CBT has proven effective in helping individuals reframe counterproductive mental loop patterns that exacerbate emotional overload. Distorted beliefs are challenged and practical strategies taught for stress reduction. CBT helps break the vicious cycle that fuels chronic stress and teaches how to see knockbacks as opportunities for growth rather than personal failures, this significantly lowers moments where self-control stumbles out of control.

5.5.3 Lifestyle and Nutrition

Addressing lifestyle factors is crucial when managing emotional overload. Regular physical exercise, a balanced diet, and sufficient sleep are paramount to a resilient stress response system.

Aerobic exercise has also been linked to reductions in cortisol levels and improvements in mood and cognitive function.

Nutritional considerations, such as ensuring adequate intake of omega-3 fatty acids, vitamins, and minerals, can also support brain function and mitigate some of the neurochemical disruptions caused by chronic stress.

5.6 Stress Physiology Management
5.6.1 Personalising Treatment

An emerging area of research is the exploration of genetic and epigenetic markers that predispose individuals to higher allostatic loads. Personalised medicine, which considers genetic variability in stress reactivity, may eventually enable tailored treatments that address individual vulnerabilities. Early identification of at-risk populations could facilitate pre-emptive strategies and customised therapies, thereby reducing the long-term impacts of chronic stress.

5.6.2 Combined and Cross-Disciplinary Approaches

The complexity of emotional overload requires a combined research approach that spans multiple disciplines, from neuroscience and psychology to endocrinology and sociology.

Cross-disciplinary studies are beginning to shed light on how cultural, environmental, and biological factors interact to influence stress responses. Such combined models will be crucial for designing comprehensive treatment programmes that not only target individual stress responses but also address systemic issues such as workplace culture and social inequality.

5.7 Turning Down the Volume
5.7.1 Recognising the Signs of Overload

A key step toward mitigating the consequences of emotional overload is early recognition. Understanding the subtle signs of chronic stress, ranging from irritability and restless nights to impaired concentration and physical symptoms like headaches, can prompt appropriate treatments sooner rather than later.

5.7.2 Balancing Stress Responses

While some degree of stress is not only inevitable but necessary for optimal performance, it is critical to strike a balance.

The goal is not to eliminate stress entirely, but to maintain it at a level where it remains a motivator rather than a destructive force. Effective stress management focuses on enhancing resilience, building the physiological and psychological capacity to adapt to and recover from stressors. In this regard, a healthy routine and good people will help keep your stress in check.

Conclusion

Emotional overload is when the body's stress response stays switched on. This can take a serious toll on both mind and body. As we've learned, when the body's stress systems stay switched on for too long, it can lead to a range of problems, from high blood pressure and weight issues to low mood and difficulty thinking clearly.

While stress is meant to help us cope in the short term, too much of it for too long becomes harmful. That fine balance between helpful and harmful stress is easily tipped in modern life.

Pressure Cooker

The good news is there are effective ways to manage it. Approaches like mindfulness, CBT, biofeedback, and simple lifestyle changes can help calm the stress response. As
research advances, especially in brain imaging and genetics, more personalised stress-management strategies are becoming possible.

In the end, understanding how stress works is key. With the right techniques, emotional overload can be managed, improving not just well-being, but performance too.

-6-

Misplaced Rage: The Spillover Effect

Introduction

Anger, as discussed earlier, is a natural response when we feel blocked or wronged.

Yet when it can't be directed at its real source, because it feels too risky or out of reach, it often gets redirected elsewhere.

This is what we've already introduced as displacement: shifting frustration onto a safer, often more vulnerable target. While this can briefly relieve tension, it frequently leads to harmful patterns that impact the wrong people.

The roots of this idea go back to early psychoanalytic theory and as covered in previous chapters, are echoed in models like the frustration–aggression hypothesis. What we see in practice is simple but troubling: when anger has nowhere to go, it finds an easier target, coworkers, family members, or marginalised groups.

So, the question becomes: why does anger go astray, and who ends up paying for it?

In this chapter, we build on earlier discussions to unpack the mechanisms behind displacement. We look at how the brain redirects emotion, how social structures shape where it lands, and how this plays out, from everyday conflicts to large-scale scapegoating. Put simply, this chapter explores how anger gets misdirected and why understanding that matters.

6.1 The Logic of Blame
6.1.1 Historical Perspectives

The concept of displacement has its roots in psychoanalytic theory. Freud and his early followers argued that when an individual is unable to direct hostile impulses toward an acceptable source, these impulses are shifted to a safer target.

In his groundbreaking work on defence mechanisms, Freud explained that displacement protects the ego by enabling the expression of repressed impulses without provoking the anxiety that direct confrontation might produce. Although early psychoanalytic interpretations were largely focused on internal conflict, the notion of displacement has since been expanded to include social and environmental factors.

Dollard and colleagues' frustration–aggression hypothesis sharpened this view, arguing that frustration reliably breeds aggression. When retaliation against the true source is blocked, by the social setting or a power imbalance, aggressive impulses do not disappear; they are displaced onto a perceived safer or substitute target. This idea shaped later research, even though experts pushed back against its simplicity. Frustration alone doesn't always spark aggression; it's more likely to do so when personal temperament and the strain of the moment tip the balance.

6.1.2 Blame, Bias & Belief

Cognitive psychology tackles displacement by asking a simple question: who or what gets the blame? Attribution theory asks: how do people explain the setbacks that occur in life?

Believe me the answer to both matters!

When frustration is chalked up to a personal flaw rather than bad luck or unfair circumstances, anger often turns inward, but not for long, sooner or later it will leak outward onto others, like toxic waste sealed in an underground storage tank that is slowly but surely corroding.

A catastrophe waiting to happen.

The mind will always seek an easier target when a source of stress feels too powerful to challenge. Snap judgements, overgeneralisation and all-or-nothing thinking easily reassign blame, and anger finds somewhere softer to land. Consider an employee heading into a performance review with a promotion at stake. The supervisor's judgment is decisive, shaping status, self-worth, and advancement. As doubts about performance surface, anxiety mounts, and owning any shortfall suddenly feels too costly. So, in the employee's mind, the narrative starts to shift. Those missed targets are blamed on a coworker's mistakes, delays, or incompetence. This sleight of hand does important psychological work as it deflects a threat, shores up self-worth, and keeps the sting of inadequacy at arm's length when the pressure is high. In doing so, anger is redirected toward the scapegoat, whose vulnerability makes them an easy target.

6.1.3 The Social Contagion of Behaviour

Social learning theory offers another framework for understanding displacement. According to Bandura's social cognitive theory, individuals learn emotional responses and coping mechanisms by observing others. Growing up with a parent who displaces frustration onto a child normalises this type of behaviour and can entrench a cycle of misdirected aggression.

The environment, whether it is family, school, or at work, plays a significant role in shaping the ways in which our anger is expressed and managed. Stressed communities often face rising crime, failing infrastructure, and economic insecurity, alongside eroding trust, scarce resources, and declining physical and mental well-being.

As the pressure mounts, short-term, reactive responses replace cooperation and long-term problem-solving. Governments and institutional hierarchies in turn often fail to address these issues. As a result, frustration accumulates and too often flows downward, landing on those with the least power or social capital.

This should not happen, hierarchies exist to absorb the pressure, not pass it on. If more investment went into basic services, transparent communication, and creating fair channels for accountability and support, those at the top could interrupt displacement and prevent frustration from being converted into harm against vulnerable groups. Without institutional support, stress in communities is displaced downward, fuelling scapegoating of lower-status groups.

6.2 Blame on the Brain
6.2.1 Judging Under Pressure

As we explored earlier through Lazarus's work, it's not just what happens that shapes how we feel, it's how we interpret it. When we feel anxious, we often focus on the discrepancy between the expected and actual outcome. If this gap is seen as a personal failure, hostile emotions, including anger, are triggered and if the source of frustration is seen as insurmountable, we may unconsciously reassign the blame to a target that is less intimidating.

This shift in attentional focus is accompanied by rapid, often unconscious, cognitive processes that simplify complex emotional experiences. Instead of engaging in a nuanced evaluation that considers multiple variables, the mind may "shortcut" the process by selecting a target based on immediate availability or vulnerability. Frustration is then offloaded onto the undeserving target, delivering instant relief, even if only more a moment.

6.2.2 Blame Games

Displacement is closely tied to attribution bias; this references our tendency to explain events in ways that protect our self-esteem. When the real source of our anger feels too risky to confront, we justify ourselves by blaming someone else. This often shows up as a familiar thinking error: we pin other people's behaviour on who they are, while overlooking the pressures or circumstances they're dealing with.

Let's consider an employee who is unable to secure a promotion because of structural issues within the organisation. Maybe you have had a similar experience? How did you deal with it?

Obviously, the wrong way would be to blame a coworker and use this as an excuse to behave in a hostile manner. This distortion of blame both redirects anger and locks in unhealthy future behavioural patterns.

6.2.3 Pulling the Emotional Brakes

Closely related to cognitive appraisals is the role of emotional regulation. Emotional regulation encompasses the strategies we often use to manage and modify our emotional experiences. In many cases, the capacity for emotion regulation is compromised by high levels of stress and frustration.

When self-regulation fails, there can be an overflow of uncontrolled emotional energy. As a result, the displaced anger finds an outlet in others or situations where inhibition is weak. Under high stress, the brain's regulatory networks, particularly those in the prefrontal cortex, are less effective at controlling reactions in the heat of the moment.

This impairment facilitates the transfer of anger from the original source to substitute targets, even if those targets are unrelated. In this way, a loss of composure can serve as the final common pathway through which displacement takes place.

6.3 Culture, Power & Blame
6.3.1 Vulnerability and Scapegoating

At the social level, certain individuals or groups may be particularly vulnerable to becoming the targets of displaced anger. These targets are often characterised by those that are socially disadvantaged, have a lower financial or educational status, or a perceived inability to retaliate. The phenomenon of scapegoating, where an individual or group is blamed for broader problems, is a common social expression of, what is called, displacement dynamics. Scapegoating serves several functions. First, it allows the aggressor to vent their emotions without confronting the real source of their frustration.

Second, by externalising blame onto a vulnerable target, the aggressor can preserve a positive self-image and avoid the cognitive dissonance that would otherwise result from acknowledging personal limitations. Social research has shown that in highly stratified societies or groups, scapegoating can serve to reinforce existing hierarchies by channelling the distress of the majority onto those with less power.

6.3.2 Mob Logic

Displacement is not solely an individual phenomenon. It can also occur on a collective level, particularly in situations where a group feels oppressed or frustrated by external circumstances.

In such scenarios, anger is often directed toward a common scapegoat as a means of unifying the group's identity and providing a tangible target for blame.

Historical examples abound, from political purges to social movements where minority groups are demonised as responsible for society's difficulties.

Collective displacement can be especially pernicious because it not only harms the immediate targets but also deepens social divisions. The process by which a group channels its collective frustration onto a marginalised group often involves media amplification and cultural narratives that legitimise the aggression.

As a result, social polarisation intensifies, and the potential for further intergroup conflict increases.

6.3.3 Family and Intimate Relationships

Within the microcosm of the family, displacement dynamics manifest in various forms of interpersonal conflict.

Let's take the example of a parent who faces stress at work, they might displace anger onto their child, a person who is inherently less likely to retaliate. Similarly, spouses might redirect frustrations arising from financial or external work pressures onto one another.

Although the targets in these scenarios are often close family members, their vulnerability in the relationship means that the displaced anger can have long-lasting emotional and psychological impacts.

Research into family dynamics has shown that such patterns of displacement are associated with poorer relationship satisfaction and increased risk of domestic violence. Therapeutic treatments that focus on communication skills and emotional regulation have been found to be effective in reducing these destructive dynamics.

6.4. Displacement in Action
6.4.1 The "Scapegoat"

Consider the case of a middle manager in a high-pressure corporate environment who is frustrated by unrealistic project deadlines and perceived lack of support from upper management.

Many of us have been in a similar situation. How did you react?

Unable to confront top management directly, the manager begins to direct their anger toward a junior colleague who has less power and is perceived as incompetent.

The manager publicly humiliates and micromanages the junior colleague, leading to a decline in team morale and productivity. Over time, the junior colleague becomes increasingly demoralised and isolated, a classic example of displacement dynamics in the workplace.

This behaviour, reinforced by a need to maintain self-esteem and avoid addressing the true sources of stress, ultimately undermines organisational performance.

Consider what you would do in a similar situation both as the manager and as the junior colleague. What action would you take to ensure a more positive and productive outcome in the workplace?

6.4.2 Misinterpreted Threat

There is an old story about a snake that slithers into a carpenter's workshop, maybe you know it already. The snake accidentally brushes against a saw, cutting itself. Startled and agitated, it turns and bites the blade.

The saw, of course, does nothing. The snake injures its mouth. Interpreting the pain as an attack, it coils around the saw in an attempt to crush it. The snake feels more intense pain as the saw cuts into its' skin. Through the night the snake continues to mistakenly interpret the relentless pain as an attack from this unknown and benign entity, the saw. As a result, the snake continues to tighten its grip on the saw with increasing anger and frustration.

In the morning, the innocuous saw still lies on the floor, inoffensive and harmless but the snake, having been cut into several pieces, is dead.

The saw never pursued or wished to harm the snake. Nonetheless the snake, unable to distinguish injury from intention, escalated the situation until it destroyed itself. Psychologically, this mirrors what professionals describe as displaced or misdirected aggression. When we experience pain and humiliation, we often search for a target rather than a cause. If we misinterpret discomfort as a deliberate attack, we may retaliate against someone, who is not even responsible for our pain. The discomfort is internal yet rather than confront that internal wound, frustration is redirected outwards as a careless collision, a sharp remark or an act of aggression.

6.4.3 Domestic Conflict

Another illustration is that of a parent who, overwhelmed by financial stress and workplace conflict, begins to display heightened irritability at home. Unable to confront the external pressures driving their frustration, the parent displaces anger onto a young child, a much less threatening target. The child's vulnerability makes them an easy outlet for misdirected aggression, resulting in harsh discipline and lasting emotional harm. Over time, the child may develop issues with trust, self-esteem, and social interactions, showing how displacement not only affects the target in the moment but can also lead to long-term developmental consequences for the "victim". Have you been in a similar situation? How did you manage these difficulties and in hindsight what would you now do differently?

6.4.4 How Societies Manufacture Guilt

When life feels unstable or things start to go wrong the worst part of human nature encourages us to look for someone or something to punish. Our fear quickly turns into anger and anger fuels the hunt for a sacrificial lamb.

The sacrificial lamb is always a weaker target or disadvantaged community, for instance, minority groups or a political enemy. In moments of economic stress, leaders latch onto our fears and often fan the flames, pointing at immigrants or other marginalised communities and blaming them for failures they had no part in. Media outrage and toxic political rhetoric pour fuel on the fire, this blame game can spiral fast, turning into real-world discrimination, violence, and social unrest. History has warned us where this leads, but even so, we are walking the same path, right now, in real time.

6.5 Displaced Anger Has Consequences
6.5.1 Psychological Impact on the Perpetrator

Dumping your anger on someone else can feel like a release in the moment, but it backfires fast! You get the release, then the crash. Lashing out at someone weaker or safer doesn't make the anger go away; it just buries it. Once the rush fades, what often sets in is guilt, shame, or a nagging sense that something's wrong. People who fall into this pattern aren't healing, they're bleeding internally.

Studies show that people who rely on this kind of emotional dumping are more likely to struggle with chronic anxiety, depression and feeling disconnected precisely because the real source of anger is never addressed. Remember, real healing begins when the true source of anger is confronted.

6.5.2 Taking the Hit

The consequences for the target of displaced anger are often severe and far-reaching. Vulnerable individuals who are repeatedly subjected to unjustified hostility often experience a range of damaging symptoms, including low self-esteem, chronic stress, and even post-traumatic stress disorder (PTSD) in extreme cases. They become worn down as self-confidence slowly erodes and stress becomes constant.

In families where children are made the scapegoat, they often carry the wound long after the blame moves on. By adolescence, it surfaces as emotional or behavioural problems and often hardens into a lifelong belief that something is wrong with them.

In the workplace, colleagues who are unjustly criticised can suffer from decreased job satisfaction, burnout, and diminished career prospects.

The social isolation and stigmatisation that often accompany being a target of displaced aggression further exacerbate these issues, leaving the team member trapped in a cycle of vulnerability, stuck, exposed and easy to blame all over again.

6.5.3 Blame is Contagious

When anger gets displaced at a collective level, the damage goes far beyond personal pain. Blame gets aimed at vulnerable groups, lines get drawn, and society starts to fracture. Scapegoating turns neighbours into enemies and keeps cycles of discrimination spinning. The demonisation of minority communities not only disrupts social cohesion but can also lead to systemic injustice and violence. History shows how easily this kind of misplaced rage can slide into riots, mass violence, and even genocide. The destabilisation of social order and the erosion of trust between community groups underscore the broader dangers of allowing displaced anger to go unchecked.

6.6 Breaking the Cycle
6.6.1 Cognitive-Behavioural Interventions

Cognitive-behavioural therapy, or CBT, helps us to catch ourselves in the act of misdirecting our anger. It teaches us to spot the mental shortcuts and distortions that push us to blame the wrong person. Through simple, practical tools, we can learn to put responsibility back where it belongs and find healthier ways to deal with stress.

Instead of feeding scapegoating, CBT helps replace those habits with more grounded, realistic thinking. Studies show it doesn't just reduce aggressive behaviour but also helps people manage their emotions better, making them far less likely to dump their anger on someone else, thereby decreasing the likelihood of displacement.

6.6.2 Emotion Regulation and Mindfulness

Mindfulness provides another solution for reducing the misdirection of anger. It will help you to slow things down instead of reacting on autopilot.

Instead of reacting instantly, you learn to notice what you're feeling without judging it or acting on it right away. This creates a space, or a moment in time, between the "feeling" of angry and the reaction.

Following a daily routine of deep breathing exercises or meditation will help calm the stress response of your body and strengthen the part of the brain that controls impulse and decision-making, bringing your thinking brain back online. In this way mindfulness acts like a brake. It interrupts the snap reactions that lead people to dump their anger on someone else and gives them a moment to pause, think, and respond in a healthier manner.

6.6.3 Social Skills and Assertiveness Training

For many individuals, learning to communicate assertively can help prevent the internalisation of frustration that later manifests as displacement. Assertiveness training focuses on developing the skills needed to express one's needs and concerns directly and respectfully rather than bottling up emotions. If we address issues at the source, we can reduce the likelihood that anger will be misdirected toward those more vulnerable.

Social skills training, particularly when combined with stress management techniques, can improve relationships and reduce the incidences of displaced aggression. These methods have been shown to successfully promote healthier conflict resolution.

6.6.4 Implementing Organisational Culture

At the broader level, organisations can play a pivotal role in reducing the factors that contribute to displacement. Workplaces that foster a supportive culture and implement fair conflict resolution procedures help reduce the environmental stressors that predispose individuals to misdirect their anger. Policies that emphasise constructive feedback over punitive criticism, as well as training programmes that focus on stress reduction and emotional intelligence, can create an environment where displaced aggression is less likely to occur. In schools' curricula that include social-emotional learning (SEL) components have been shown to improve students' coping strategies and reduce incidences of bullying and scapegoating.

6.6.5 Bringing Communities Together

Addressing displacement within communities means fostering unity instead of division. Public awareness, open dialogue, and policies that reduce inequality can counter harmful narratives and prevent scapegoating. When people feel valued and included, they're less likely to direct frustration at others, helping reduce the broader social impact of displaced anger.

6.7 Turning Insight into Action
6.7.1 Across Time and Cultures

Displaced aggression is complicated, and we still don't fully understand how it plays out over time. We need more long-term studies that follow individuals and groups to see how these patterns start, shift, and stick. We also need more cross-cultural research, since ideas about who counts as "vulnerable" and how anger gets expressed vary widely from place to place.

Getting a better handle on these differences could help create new approaches that actually fit the cultural realities people live in, rather than relying on one-size-fits-all solutions.

6.7.2 Changing Society for the Better

Taking society, research into displacement dynamics has critical implications for government policymaking. Understanding how systemic inequalities and cultural narratives contribute to scapegoating can guide policy makers to write public policy aimed at reducing social polarisation.

It would also be interesting to explore how regulations, such as anti-discrimination laws and educational reforms, could have a measurable impact on reducing displaced aggression in communities.

We hope that these insights can help create a more inclusive world that mitigate the conditions under which displacement thrives.

6.7.3 Breaking the Chain

As we have discussed, displacement is what happens when anger aimed at a real threat gets redirected toward a safer target.

Displacement is shaped by the way we think, how our brains respond to stress, and the social setting we are in.

Spotting early warning signs, like snapping more easily, twisted thinking, or regularly blaming others with less power, is the first step to stopping our anger from landing in the wrong place.

6.7.4 Combining Multi-Level Treatments

Addressing displacement requires input at multiple levels. On an individual basis, cognitive-behavioural techniques and mindfulness offer approaches for reining in impulsive anger. At the interpersonal level, assertiveness training and social skills development can reduce the tendency to direct aggression toward easy targets.

Moreover, organisational and institutional policies that foster inclusivity and fair treatment can diminish the external pressures that fuel displacement. The convergence of these approaches has the potential to not only reduce the harmful consequences of displaced aggression but also enhance overall emotional resilience and social cohesion.

6.7.5 The Way Forward

The redirection of anger onto vulnerable targets poses severe implications for both individual well-being and broader social dynamics. While displacement may serve as a temporary defence mechanism, its long-term consequences, ranging from conflict and psychological distress to systemic social inequality, demand serious attention.

We, as a society, must better understand displacement and improve ways to prevent it by offering supportive and inclusive environments. Only in this way will people feel empowered to manage anger which in turn will change a harmful impulse into an opportunity for growth and healing.

Emotional growth does not stop on our 18th birthday when we are legally recognised as adults.

We may not understand it but all of us can heal our wounds. In chasing greater things, we may have neglected our inner child, unhealed and unheard, but it is still possible to reconnect as our circumstances change. In adulthood we are still capable of emotional evolution, for instance, maybe after tossing and turning for a couple of sleepless nights we finally start to overcome those outbursts of envy or start to understand why we are so embarrassed when praised.

During another week, we forgive ourselves for something that's been weighing on our minds or finally understand the dynamics of a relationship that has been puzzling us.

These moments are quiet. No one applauds them. But they matter. They mark inner growth, and even though we are grown up, a small part of us, still silently hopes that someone might notice.

So, keep this in mind, we notice and applaud you!

Conclusion

In conclusion, understanding displacement dynamics is not only vital for psychologists and neuroscientists but also for educators, organisational leaders, and policy makers.

The insights gleaned from studies in this area underscore the need for comprehensive, multi-level strategies to reduce the incidence of displaced aggression. When anger is redirected onto the vulnerable, the consequences are profound and far-reaching, but with targeted measures, it is possible to break this cycle, protect those at risk, and foster healthier communities overall.

-7-

When Self Worth Starts to Crumble

Introduction

Self-esteem is basically how much you like and trust yourself.

The problem?

When you keep missing your own, or everyone else's, sky-high standards, it takes a hit, and over time, those hits add up.

That's when self-doubt crashes the party and relationships start to wobble. In a world obsessed with achievement, that gap between expectation and reality is everywhere, and those repeated faltering moments will slowly chip away at how we see ourselves.

Let's take a look at how this happens, and more importantly, how to rebuild confidence without needing to be perfect.

7.1 The Nature of Self-Esteem
7.1.1 Confidence & Self Worth

Self-esteem refers to a person's overall sense of self-worth, encompassing both how abilities are evaluated and how well one accepts personal flaws.

When self-esteem is high, we tend to show greater confidence, resilience, and a willingness to engage with challenges. When it is low, it often manifests as self-doubt, feelings of inadequacy, and heightened self-criticism.

Importantly, self-esteem is not fixed; it shifts with experience and is shaped by social and cultural influences.

As shown in measures like Rosenberg's Self-Esteem Scale, higher self-esteem is linked to better relationships and well-being, while lower self-esteem is tied to anxiety, depression, and less favourable outcomes.

7.1.2 Why Self Esteem Can Make or Break Us

Through a positive lens, self-esteem can work like a shield, it helps us handle everyday stress and to keep going when things get difficult. It fuels optimism and persistence.

But it's also fragile.

When there's a constant gap between how we think we should be doing and how we're actually doing, self-esteem takes a knock.

Repeated feelings of inability, whether caused by outside barriers or personal limits, can slowly wear down our self-worth.

The erosion of self-esteem is not an instantaneous process; it often develops gradually through repeated experiences where self-expectations are not met. Each knock can start to feel like proof that something is "wrong" with us.
Over time, those thoughts can harden into a deep belief that we're simply not good enough.

7.2 The Weight of Repeated Failure
7.2.1 The Role of Unmet Self-Expectations

Personal inability can be defined as the perception that one cannot meet one's own performance standards or societies expectations.

When we set high self-standards, whether realistic or not, the gap between what one aspires to achieve and what is attained becomes significant. According to self-discrepancy theory (Higgins, 1987), mismatches between the "actual self", one's perceived current state, and the "ideal self", one's aspirations, produce discomfort and distress including feelings of shame and disappointment. When these feelings of despair accumulate, they weaken overall self-esteem. Specifically taking an example of a student who consistently scores below a set standard they may begin to consider themselves as less capable, leading to diminished academic self-concept and even eventual disengagement.

7.2.2 The Stories We Tell Ourselves

A key cognitive mechanism involved in the erosion of self-esteem is cognitive dissonance. When we experience an inconsistency between our expectations and our performance, the resulting dissonance can be psychologically distressing. To reduce this dissonance, many engage in finding explanations that in reality are self-defeating.

Instead of blaming setbacks on circumstances, we turn them inward and see them as proof that we just "aren't good at this." This kind of thinking, often called a "fixed mindset," as opposed to a "growth mindset" (Dweck, 2006), reinforces the belief that one is inherently inadequate. Attributional style is critical in determining emotional responses to failure. Individuals with a self-critical or pessimistic attributional style tend to interpret setbacks as global and permanent. An employee fails to secure a promotion and believes the failure is due solely to personal incompetence rather than other external factors, their self-esteem is likely to suffer. After a while, such an attributional style can create a self-fulfilling prophecy whereby expectations of failure lead to reduced motivation and increasingly poor performance.

7.2.3 Perfectionism and Rumination

Perfectionism represents an extreme form of self-imposed expectation. This ultimately leads to a person refusing, point blank; to accept any deviation from flawlessness and as a result these perfectionistic individuals are more vulnerable to the effects of eroded self-esteem when faced with inevitable human error. When a single mistake is interpreted as catastrophic, people ruminate on their shortcomings. This rumination becomes repetitive and passive, focusing solely on feelings of distress and their cause, ultimately leading to a prolonged low mood and continuing self-criticism.

This persistent rumination then undermines a person's ability to resolve problems and eventually contributes to additional chronic stress. In academic and professional settings, where perfectionism is often inadvertently rewarded, the pressure to be flawless can lead to an endless loop of self-blame and diminished self-worth.

7.2.4 Comparison – Making It Louder!

When ability is in question, social comparisons become a double-edged sword. Observing the success of others can motivate improvement; however, when the comparisons are unfavourable, they can intensify feelings of inadequacy.

Take a competitive workplace, it's easy to stack up your wins against your coworkers', but how does it feel when you come up short?

If, these comparisons consistently highlight one's shortcomings, self-esteem will erode, rapidly. This is especially true in a world filled with curated images of success and perfection, which create unrealistic benchmarks.

7.3 How Comparison Kills Confidence
7.3.1 Identity & Perceived Failure

One's self-concept is intricately linked to ability. If success is part of your identity, failure just doesn't disappoint, it feels like an attack on who you are. This is particularly true in domains where personal worth is closely tied to achievement. Failure is more than just getting something wrong; it becomes a repudiation of one's very identity.

When an athlete's sense of self is built around winning, an unexpected loss can shake them to the core. Struggling to accept the gap between who they think they are and what just happened can crush their confidence and even trigger depression or anxiety. When success in one area defines your worth, failure is devastating.

7.3.2 The Inner Rules That Work Against Us

Our core beliefs shape how we see the world and everything that happens in it. If you believe deep down that you're not good enough, your mind starts twisting events to fit that story.

These patterns warp new experiences to fit the same story, often reinforcing the feeling of not being good enough. As difficulties continue to crop up, that belief becomes stronger, diminishing self-esteem. Over time, it will lead to feelings of worthlessness and an increased risk of suffering from depression.

The cognitive vulnerability model of depression argues that unhelpful thinking patterns, when triggered by stress, can cause a sharp drop in self-esteem. As these patterns take hold, self-worth deteriorates, creating a cycle that is challenging to break.

7.3.3 The Cost of Emotional Spirals

The way we respond to failure can either protect or undermine our self-esteem. Yet, when people struggle to manage their emotions, even minor difficulties can trigger overwhelming feelings of despair.

When a person is unable to manage their emotions, in other words when emotional dysregulation occurs, the impact of impulsiveness and prolonged rumination will lead to intense mood swings and contribute significantly to the erosion of their self-esteem. At this point, the brain's emotional control system goes offline, and high stress walks through the open door.

When these control systems are weak, it's harder to reframe the hard and high bumps on life's long road, so those bad feelings linger and self-doubt is constantly reinforced.

7.4 Playing It Out
7.4.1 When Marks Become Identity

Consider the case of a high-achieving student who, throughout primary and secondary education, received constant praise for academic excellence. As expectations rose, the student internalised the belief that their worth was synonymous with academic performance. Upon entering college, a setting characterised by greater competition and more complex challenges, the student experienced a series of setbacks, such as lower-than-expected grades on crucial exams.

These failures were not viewed as isolated incidents but were interpreted as proof of a personal flaw. The cumulative effect was a gradual erosion of self-esteem, leading to feelings of hopelessness and withdrawal.

As Eileen Gu mentioned in one of her interviews, at the Milan-Cortina Olympics 2026, when you keep winning medals, people start expecting gold every time and although this is something she acknowledges she refuses to let it define her mindset. A narrow achievement-contingent self-esteem framework can leave someone disillusioned and unsure of who they really are when confronted with the inevitable realities of failure.

7.5 Measuring Up
7.5.1 Who Are You?

Many professionals come to define themselves almost entirely by how well they perform at work. Take a senior marketing executive who has built their reputation on successful campaigns and steady promotions. After years of praise and strong results, a string of underperforming projects, or a sudden restructuring, can trigger a serious identity shake-up.

A common scenario such as a marketer who once thought, *"I'm the best at what I do",* begins to reinterpret setbacks as a personal failure. Missed targets or critical feedback start to feel less like part of the job and more like proof of incompetence. That shift fuels anxiety, second-guessing, and hesitation, which often leads to underperformance, creating a vicious cycle. Eventually, the damage to confidence follows them home and self-doubt spills into personal life, affecting relationships, motivation, health and overall well-being.

Studies in occupational psychology highlight the importance of a balanced sense of self, one that isn't entirely tied to the job. In the long-term this will protect confidence, improve resilience, and build strong mental health.

7.5.2 When Insecurity Breaks Connection

When people start to feel incapable, the blow to self-confidence often spills into their relationships. Someone who feels constantly "not good enough" may pull away from others or get defensive when they receive feedback. Sometimes, they are so expectant of criticism or rejection that they act in ways that actually bring it about. These strained relationships only reinforce the feeling that something is wrong with them.

Family dynamics provide a microcosm of this process. A parent with diminished self-esteem may be less emotionally available or more prone to conflict, which not only affects their own mental health but also has lasting adverse effects on their children. Children raised in environments where parents exhibit low self-esteem are more likely to develop insecure attachment styles and struggle with self-confidence later in life.

7.6 Turn Around
7.6.1 Give Yourself a Break

Self-compassion, a concept popularised by Kristin Neff, involves treating oneself with kindness, understanding, and patience in the face of perceived shortcomings. Practices aimed at cultivating self-compassion have been found to significantly improve self-esteem by helping individuals move away from harsh self-criticism.

Practices such as guided self-compassion meditation and reflective journaling can help reframe personal failure as part of the shared human experience, reducing the severity of the inner critic. Those who practice self-compassion are less likely to experience long-term emotional distress after setbacks and are more resilient in the face of new challenges.

7.6.2 Stop Arguing with Yourself

Mindfulness also teaches the skill of paying attention to thoughts and feelings without judgment which helps to stop the cycle of overthinking after a setback. Acceptance and Commitment Therapy (ACT) is one such method that combines mindfulness with strategies for accepting misguided feelings, thereby reducing their impact on self-esteem.

Through techniques such as cognitive diffusion, where individuals learn to see their thoughts as transient mental events, ACT helps in breaking the cycle of self-criticism and fosters a more balanced view of personal ability.

7.6.3 Turning the Setback into Progress

How people think about ability shapes how they interpret success and failure, Dweck (1988). Later Dweck expanded this theory in 2006 and demonstrated how fixed and growth mindsets influence motivation, persistence, emotions and responses to setbacks.

Bottom Line, if you believe ability is fixed, failure is hugely demoralising and feels more personal. If you believe skills can grow, setbacks feel more like lessons than a final verdict. Teaching a growth mindset helps people to understand that mistakes are a part of life, a part of learning to live, not proof that they're not good enough. That said, we should always try our best, to put our best foot forward, so to speak. Organisations that incorporate growth mindset training have demonstrated improvements in self-confidence and persistence. Shifting the focus from innate ability to continued learning and progress, helps protect self-esteem from the corrosive effects of several bumps along the road.

7.6.4 Stronger Together

Social comparison and relationship stress, as we know, can slowly chip away at confidence. Alone time is great and we all need some of that but, spend too long on your own and the brain may go rogue!

It is important to have a strong support network of friends and family. Group therapy, mentoring, and peer support also offer fresh perspectives and alternative routes for receiving encouragement, honest feedback and helping to rebuild a healthier sense of self.

We are more resilient to stress and more capable of maintaining positive self-esteem when we stand together. Even if we repeatedly fall, there will be some-one to support us as we pick ourselves up.

7.7 Turning Insight into Change
7.7.1 Combining What Works

No single method is likely to provide a complete solution for the erosion of self-esteem resulting from perceived worthlessness.

Instead, a multifaceted approach that integrates cognitive-behavioural strategies, mindfulness, self-compassion, and social support is most promising. Blended programmes that combine these methods, often tailored to the unique needs of the patient, can produce compounding benefits, enhancing both immediate relief and long-term resilience.

7.7.2 What Society Gets Wrong

While individual actions are critical, it is also important to acknowledge institutional and social influences that contribute to the erosion of self-esteem.

Cultural expectations that equate self-worth with success and achievement create an environment in which failure is stigmatised. One can go from being a "Winner" to a "Loser" in a flash, like rotting fruit hurtling to the ground. Institutional changes can challenge outdated cultural narratives and promote a more balanced view of ability. One that values effort and consistency alongside results, supporting healthier, happier people.

7.8 Toward a More Resilient Self
7.8.1 Restructuring Self-Identity

Restoring self-esteem often involves a fundamental reconfiguration of one's identity. This reconfiguration entails shifting from an identity that is entirely contingent on performance outcomes to one that values intrinsic qualities such as effort, creativity, and compassion.

Methods that promote a more holistic self-concept, not solely defined by success, can provide lasting benefits. Both therapy and personal development programmes can facilitate this change by encouraging us, as individuals, to explore and affirm diverse aspects of our identity.

7.8.2 Embracing Imperfection as a Strength

An essential component of rebuilding self-esteem is learning to accept imperfection. Recognising that failure is a normal and unavoidable part of life can help mitigate the harsh self-judgments that contribute to low esteem. Cultivating self-compassion and developing a growth mindset work hand in hand to foster an attitude that views setbacks as opportunities for learning and personal development rather than as definitive judgments of one's value.

In doing so, we can build a resilient foundation that buffers against future disappointments.

7.8.3 Emotional Education Without Prejudice

In elite cultural circles, no genre is looked down on more than self-help. The phrase itself has become shorthand for fluff, nonsense, and scams. Honestly, a lot of the criticism isn't wrong.

The covers are loud and the promises ridiculous but throwing out the whole idea that humans sometimes need comfort, guidance, and emotional education is a strangely harsh prejudice.

Earlier cultures were far more relaxed about this. The great Greek and Roman thinkers, people like Aristotle, Seneca, Cicero, and Marcus Aurelius, were openly in the business of helping people live better.

Their philosophy was practical. It dealt with fear, purpose, love, anger, and how to stay sane in a difficult world. That tradition didn't stop in antiquity. Montaigne's *Essays* are basically a handbook for understanding our messy minds and learning how to live with peace and honesty. Proust, too, was doing something similar: *In Search of Lost Time* is, at heart, a long meditation on how not to waste our lives and how to really live them while we're here.

So, the problem isn't self-help itself. It's what the genre is often turned into. At its best, there are few tasks more serious than helping people feel less confused, less alone, and more able to live healthy, happy and fulfilled lives.

The way forward isn't to sneer at self-help, but to rescue it: to take emotional education seriously, and to do it with intelligence, depth, and dignity.

Educators, leaders and clinicians should continue to provide one to one support but in addition it would be beneficial to foster settings that nurture healthy self-esteem, for example, developing strategies and policies that emphasise personal growth and inclusiveness.

A shift in the narrative that switches from all demanding perfection to instead valuing perseverance.

In this way we can help safeguard against the possible damaging impacts of failure and create a more resilient community.

Conclusion

Feeling incapable can slowly eat away at self-esteem, with serious consequences for mental health and quality of life.

This chapter has shown how high expectations, when they're not met, can set off a chain reaction of counterproductive thoughts, emotions, and behaviours that steadily erode self-worth. When failure is taken as proof of "not being good enough," it can lead to deep and lasting self-doubt.

Patterns like perfectionism, overthinking, and constant comparison make rough patches harder than they should be. We need to remember that these consequences don't happen in isolation, they're shaped by the systems and cultures that surround us.

The good news?

Change is possible.

-8-

Mind in Conflict:
When Identity Cracks

Introduction

We, as humans, usually like to think we've got ourselves all figured out, our values, our abilities, that polished image we have spent a lifetime building. Then life steps in and says, *"Not quite."*

When reality clashes with the carefully curated version of ourselves, it doesn't feel so comfortable anymore. That is cognitive dissonance knocking at the door!

In simple terms, it's the mental difficulty of holding two conflicting beliefs at once, especially when who we think we are doesn't match what just happened.

Seriously?

At that point, our minds start scrambling to try and make sense of it all. Unfortunately, not always in the healthiest of ways.

8.1 Inner Conflict & the Battle for Consistency
8.1.1 The Stranger Within Us

We don't know ourselves nearly as well as we think. We live inside our minds, yet we're usually the last to understand what's driving us. There's no clean way in, so we stay confused, reactive and emotional without really knowing why.

Pressure Cooker

We wreck relationships, misjudge our abilities and walk around with a background hum of anxiety and "are you for real?"

Sadly, what we don't face doesn't go away. It mutates.

Ambition becomes panic. Envy turns toxic. Anger blows up. Sadness sinks deep. If we ignore our inner life long enough, it will jump out and hit us with compulsions, revulsions, numbness or despair.

This is the cost of ignorance.

Socrates believed enlightenment begins with knowing yourself, but sadly we are very bad at it. The ancient sceptics caught on long ago, Pyrrho often joked that the average pig is cleverer, kinder and happier than the average human. Our minds lie to us constantly, skewed by hunger, exhaustion, desire and mood swings.

Maturity starts when we stop trusting our own thoughts. Doubting your inner story is not a weakness, it is intelligence.

Emotional scepticism may be the only defence we have against the damage we're otherwise guaranteed to do. Yet frustration is not purely destructive. In many situations it serves an important purpose.

It signals that something in our environment, our expectations, or our behaviour needs adjustment. In its constructive form, frustration motivates persistence, problem-solving, and growth.

The challenge lies in recognising the difference between productive and destructive frustration and understanding the triggers that cause one to transform into the other.

8.1.2 The Illusion of Self

At the heart of cognitive inconsistency lies the conflict between a person's self-image (the "ideal self") and the reality of their experiences (the "actual self"). Self-discrepancy theory, as articulated by Higgins (1987), explains that discrepancies between the actual self, the ideal self, and the ought self, often lead to dysphoric emotions such as disappointment, shame and guilt. When a person's achievements or behaviours fall short of their ideal standards, the resulting dissonance is particularly painful because it undermines the very core of personal identity. Elena is a senior engineer known for her precision and reliability. During a high-profile project, a miscalculation in her design leads to an unexpected delay and requires revision by a colleague. Although the error is quickly corrected, Elena experiences feelings of embarrassment and disappointment, because the mistake conflicts with her self-image as a prudent and careful professional. To ease this tension, she attributes the error to unrealistic deadlines and reframes the incident.

Confident, Elena begins   A costly error is discovered   Elena searches for a way to cope

8.1.3 The Mind Demands Resolution

A key component of cognitive dissonance theory is the idea that the discomfort arising from incongruence motivates us, as individuals, to engage in various strategies to reduce this inconsistency.

These strategies often involve several approaches. Some people may reframe their beliefs, adjusting standards or redefining failure.

They might change their behaviour to improve performance or justify their actions. Others simply avoid information or situations that heighten the inconsistency.

Finally, they may rationalise, offering explanations that cast the situation in a more favourable light.

These strategies, while effective in the short term for alleviating the inner conflict, can sometimes lead to dysfunctional patterns.

If the conflict is resolved by trying to "explain it away", in other words self-justification, rather than genuine change, the underlying issues will remain unresolved.

Let's take the example of a small business owner who defines himself as competent, responsible, and personally accountable for his company's success.

When a strategic decision results in disappointing sales, the outcome threatens his core identity rather than simply reflecting a bad result.

Starting out. Confident Sam.   Results very disappointing.   Sam searches for a way to cope

The mismatch between who he believes he is and what occurred produces an internal conflict, often felt as a sense that something is not quite right or self-doubt.

To restore a coherent sense of self, he may be tempted to shift responsibility onto things outside his control, minimise the importance of the outcome, or reinterpret the failure rather than attributing it to his poor judgment.

8.2 The Engine of the Divided Self
8.2.1 The Mind's Inconsistency Alarm

As we learned earlier in chapter three, cognitive dissonance arises when our beliefs and actions don't align. Now we will take a closer look at how that conflict unfolds and why, at times, it can be so difficult to resolve. In the beginning, the process is largely unconscious, under our radar so to speak, but when something we do clashes with how we see ourselves, the brain quickly picks up on it.

Studies show areas like the anterior cingulate cortex (ACC) responsible for error and conflict detection are activated (Botvinick et al., 2004). The brain flags the incongruence and signals that something needs immediate attention.

Taking, for example, a young corporate lawyer who prides himself on being ethical, principled, and committed to the rule of law. Early in his career, he joins a prestigious firm where professional success is closely tied to client retention and billable hours. During a high-stakes case, he is instructed by senior partners to structure an agreement that, while technically legal, is deliberately opaque and designed to mislead a less sophisticated opposing party.

A Young Lawyer Faces Ethical Dilemma

A young lawyer who values ethics & fairness

A firm pressures him to engage in a misleading contract.

He rationalises to ease inner conflict.

Although no laws are explicitly broken, the practice conflicts with his internal standards of fairness and transparency. He recognises that refusing to comply could jeopardise his position at the firm and stall his career. He agrees to proceed; however, this forces him to act in ways that contradict his self-image as an ethical professional.

This discrepancy between his moral identity, "I am an honest lawyer", and his behaviour, "I am facilitating a misleading practice", produces cognitive dissonance, experienced as unease, guilt, and persistent self-doubt.

To manage the distress of this inner conflict, he begins to rationalise, or rather deceive himself, he finds excuses for the whitewash and morally disengages from the situation, telling himself that the responsibility lies with the partners, that such practices are industry norms or that his role is merely advisory rather than moral. In the short-term, these justifications help him to appease his conscience, but at a cost.

8.2.2 The Cost of Conflict

When things don't line up, the strain isn't just cognitive, it's emotional. When evidence challenges how we see ourselves, strong feelings like anxiety, guilt, shame, or anger can surface. These emotions are warning signals, telling us that something important about who we are is threatened. The more central the belief is to our identity, the stronger the emotional reaction will be.

When an artist who believes themselves to be uniquely talented receives harsh criticism, it can feel very personal because it challenges their identity.

The emotional upheaval makes the inner conflict impossible to ignore and pushes the person to quickly restore a sense of balance between who they believe they are and what reality reflects. In the long run if these emotional clashes are unresolved, they can turn into ongoing stress that gradually undermines overall well-being.

8.2.3 The Brain's CEO

Brain scans have shed light on how the brain processes cognitive dissonance. In addition to the anterior cingulate cortex (ACC), the prefrontal cortex (PFC), otherwise known as "The Brain's CEO" plays a crucial role in regulating responses to conflict. The PFC is involved in decision-making, planning, and the inhibition of impulsive responses.

When faced with incongruence, a well-functioning PFC will help us to evaluate the inconsistent information, weigh possible resolutions, and choose a path to reduce the conflict effectively. However, under conditions of high emotional arousal or chronic stress, the regulatory capacity of the PFC is compromised. This impairment can make it more difficult for us to engage in reflective thinking, leading us to resolve the incompatibility through quick, but sometimes inappropriate, strategies such as moral disengagement, finding excuses, self-justification or denial.

These neurobiological insights explain why, at times, all of us, when under prolonged pressure or emotional strain may repeatedly find ourselves stuck in cycles of self-justification and self-loathing.

8.3 Let the Evidence Speak for Itself
8.3.1 Classically Congruent

Early research on cognitive congruence primarily relied on behavioural experiments that illustrated how people change their attitudes or beliefs to reduce anxiety.

One of the initial pioneering experiments was the "induced compliance" study, in which participants were asked to perform a task that conflicted with their original attitudes. The participants who engaged in behaviour that was contrary to their beliefs, for instance, writing a persuasive essay advocating a position they did not agree with, later changed their minds to match their behaviour and reduce internal conflict (Festinger & Carlsmith, 1959).

These groundbreaking experiments demonstrated, what was called, the insufficient-justification effect. In the experiment, participants were asked to say a boring task was enjoyable. Those paid $1 felt increased cognitive dissonance compared to those paid $20, because $1 wasn't enough to justify going against their self-image: "I'm honest, but I lied."

Participants reduced the resulting discomfort by changing their own beliefs, later reporting that the task was relatively more enjoyable than they had first imagined.

In contrast, the twenty-dollar payment provided a clear external reason for lying, which reduced dissonance and therefore reduced attitude change. This pattern suggests that cognitive dissonance, and the pressure to resolve it, is shaped by the balance between inconsistent behaviour and the availability of external justification for that behaviour.

8.3.2 The Evolution of Self Image & Dissonance

Cognitive dissonance is important to self-esteem when it feels like a threat to who we are.

In the short term, people usually protect their self-worth by justifying their actions, changing their attitudes, or focusing on other positive parts of themselves. If you resolve inner struggles by truly shifting your beliefs or values, it can help you feel better about yourself.

On the other hand, if the conflict, cognitive dissonance, is repeatedly avoided or rationalised, this may falsely preserve a sense of consistency, but it will gradually undermine self-esteem as alarm bells continue to ring in the background.

Although theory strongly supports this idea, evidence in the long-term is still limited but one thing's certain: it's not how often cognitive dissonance shows up, but how you handle it that impacts your self-esteem. This has been confirmed through research that tracked people who repeatedly experienced a gap between their self-expectations and actual outcomes.

The result, their unresolved dissonance led to a persistent decline in their own sense of value. Further work-related studies have illustrated that employees who receive conflicting messages about their competence, such as being praised for effort yet receiving poor performance evaluations, can also experience chronic cognitive dissonance. Again, over the longer term, the inability to reconcile these conflicting messages contributes to burnout, decreased job satisfaction, and lower self-esteem (Davis & Roberts, 2021).

8.3.3 How the Brain Resolves Inner Conflict

More recently neuroimaging techniques have been adopted to observe the brain's response to cognitive dissonance in real time. Functional magnetic resonance imaging (fMRI) studies have confirmed that the ACC and PFC are consistently activated when participants are confronted with inconsistent information about themselves. Experiments were conducted asking participants to evaluate statements that either aligned or conflicted with their self-perception. When the statement strongly conflicted with the participants self-perception, they experienced greater unease and due to this psychological conflict, created by the statements, the magnitude of brain activity was increased which often led to a more likely chance that the participant adjusted their views afterwards (van Veen et al., 2009).

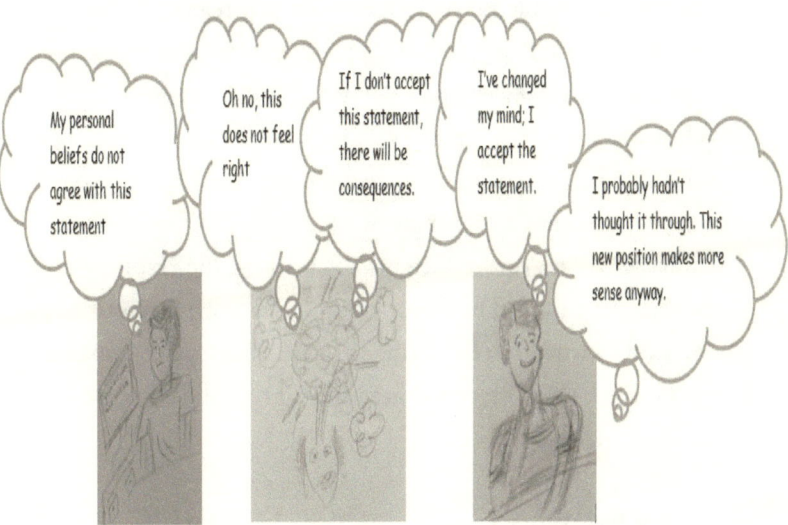

These findings suggest that cognitive dissonance is not just a concept, but something that is reflected in measurable brain activity.

The results also suggest that methods aimed at strengthening prefrontal regulation, such as mindfulness training, could potentially ameliorate the detrimental effects of dissonance by enhancing the brain's capacity to manage conflicting thoughts.

8.4 When Self-Image Contrasts with Reality
8.4.1 Academia: The Struggle to Reconcile Aspiration with Outcome

Cognitive dissonance commonly arises in academia where professional identity is closely tied to performance and evaluation.

Let's consider an assistant professor who has built his self-concept around being a capable and productive researcher. After dedicating several years to a research project, he submits his work to a highly regarded academic journal, only to have it rejected. The feedback provided is brief and does not clearly explain the reasons for the decision, creating a conflict between his self-image as a competent scholar and the apparent devaluation of his work. To protect his self-esteem, he may initially attribute the rejection to external factors such as reviewer bias or editorial priorities. If these explanations do not reduce his discomfort, the resulting cognitive dissonance can lead to various outcomes: increased effort and revision to restore self-worth, or, if the dissonance remains unresolved, growing self-doubt and a gradual decline in professional confidence.

8.4.2 When Work Challenges Your Identity

In professional environments, cognitive dissonance can be particularly damaging when individuals' work-related self-image is challenged by objective feedback.

Let's look at the example of an employee who prides themselves on being an innovative and efficient problem-solver but is met with critical performance reviews that highlight deficiencies in their work. The contrast between the employee's self-perception and the evaluative reality generates dissonance that must be resolved. Often, this resolution involves either ignoring or rationalising away the critical feedback.

Alternatively, the employee could choose to accept the feedback and invest extra effort in professional development to align their performance with their self-image. However, if any of these strategies fail and the internal conflict is not addressed, these issues can lead to decreased job satisfaction, burnout, or even a complete crisis of identity.

8.4.3 When Relationships Trigger Self-Doubt

Within personal relationships, discrepancies between self-image and actual behaviour can have particularly intimate consequences. Let's consider an individual who sees themselves as a caring and reliable friend, but who repeatedly fails to meet the expectations of others, perhaps by cancelling plans or not providing support when needed.

The resulting dissonance, between how one views oneself and the reactions of close others, can lead to deep-seated self-doubt. Over time, this repeated pattern may cause the individual to withdraw from relationships entirely, reinforcing a cycle of loneliness and poor self-image. This is just one example of how cognitive dissonance in our personal lives can contribute to the erosion of self-esteem and emotional well-being.

8.4.4 System Crash

As humans we are exceptionally competent at soldiering on. We put the needs of the world before our own, oddly committed to the expectations of others and powering on with priorities not defined by us.

We keep showing up and doing what we've been told to do. "It's always been this way." "It's tradition." "It's our culture." If you can't, or won't, stay inside the carefully gilded cage that's been polished over centuries, then somehow, you're the problem. There must be something wrong with you.

Of course, there's nothing inherently wrong with tradition or culture. They give us structure, belonging and protection. We, as humans, have always survived by sticking together, hunting, gathering, building, supporting one another, but we are also creatures who evolve. Nevertheless, sometimes evolution requires a pause. A breath. A moment of reflection.

Change for the sake of change is not wisdom, but change that evolves from thoughtful reflection, from understanding when something no longer fits, is not betrayal.

It's growth.

Often, we do not stop but continue to execute this illusion day in and day out flawlessly for years until one day we burn out. The signs of burn out can be anything from not being able to get out of bed, social anxiety, paranoia, loss of appetite or losing control over our body.

We go wildly off script and do something completely out of character, something audacious and possibly even delightfully improper, surprising everyone, even ourselves! We gleefully hurl that stick into what has become the perfectly, spinning routine of our lives, bringing to an abrupt halt that flawless performance we have executed for years like a programmed machine. We can pretend to be fine whilst carefully navigating stressful jobs with contradictory and unreasonable leadership. We continue to shrug off disappointing relationships, family betrayals, as if tiptoeing on a floor of eggshells and then there is the ever-present existential dread of another morning alarm.

We compute this ritual day after day with courtesy and a smile whilst internally screaming, as if nurturing a Chestburster in the second stage of the Xenomorph life cycle. The larval form slowly growing inside us after implantation by a random Facehugger.

Then, one day, to our total astonishment, this pocket-sized alien frantically pulls the emergency exit.

Coping isn't just a skill we develop in childhood; it becomes part of our personality, until one day the system crashes. We throw a tantrum because the Wi-Fi doesn't work. We start staring at our computer thinking, "What happened to my life?"

If we have a breakdown, although it is, of course, extremely inconvenient, we are not going insane, it's accumulated honesty. We can only suppress our needs for so long before our psyche grabs a microphone and shouts, "I'm resigning from this version of myself that you have created."

A breakdown is inconvenient and humbling, but it is not a weakness. It is a reset.

It signals the uncomfortable realisation that being infinitely functional and genuinely fulfilled do not always go hand in hand.

8.4.5 Judgement Under the Digital Spotlight

The advent of social media has transformed the way we build and compare self-image. We are all familiar with the carefully curated representations of success and beauty on social media platforms like Instagram or Facebook. It pushes some people to chase "perfect" lives, others to watch and judge, and some to project envy with harsh comments, forgetting that no one's life is actually perfect.

If people do feel that their lives are falling short in some way due to these highly edited representations, then cognitive dissonance may arise. The conflict between one's everyday reality and the idealised images encountered online can lead to feelings of inadequacy, low self-worth and possibly depression. Studies have shown that excessive use of social media is correlated with lower self-esteem, largely because of these constant and often unconscious, comparisons.

The most important thing is to focus on building your life, one that supports your health, happiness, and goals. One that enriches the people you care about. Your path is your own, and it doesn't need to look like anyone else's. Social media can inspire and entertain when kept in perspective, but following someone else's life too closely can pull you away from your own purpose. Take inspiration from people you admire, learn from mentors, but always stay true to the direction that feels right for you.

Never replace your own direction.

8.5 Turn Inner Conflict into Growth
8.5.1 Cognitive Behavioural Approaches

Through this journey, we have learned that Cognitive Behavioural Therapy CBT helps to close the gap between how we see ourselves and reality. It teaches us to reframe setbacks, not as a reflection of our worth, but as part of learning and growth. Research shows that over time it reduces distress, helps us to better manage our emotions and improves our self-perception. If we keep getting discouraging feedback, CBT helps us not take it personally. We focus on what to improve and make a plan, easing any anguish and helping us to rebuild confidence.

8.5.2 Secure in Who You Are

Self-affirmation theory (Steele, 1988) proposes that we can reduce dissonance by reaffirming core personal values that are unrelated to the source of conflict. If a person's self-image, for instance, as an ethical individual is challenged by a failure at work, affirming other aspects of their identity, such as being a supportive friend or a creative thinker, can help buffer the adverse impact of that a disconnect. Strategies based on self-affirmation have shown promise in a variety of settings, including academic, occupational, and interpersonal.

In one study, college students who engaged in self-affirmation exercises were better able to cope with the stress of receiving poor grades, as these exercises bolstered their overall self-integrity (Cohen et al., 2006). When the basis of self-worth is broadened, self-affirmation techniques can provide us with multiple sources of self-esteem, thereby making our self-concept less vulnerable to isolated failures.

8.5.3 Staying Grounded

Mindfulness offers another promising avenue for mitigating the distress of cognitive dissonance. It involves the cultivation of non-judgmental awareness of present-moment experiences, allowing us to observe our thoughts and feelings without becoming overwhelmed. Through practices such as meditation and deep-breathing exercises, we can learn to accept discrepancies between self-image and reality without resorting to harsh self-criticism.

It has been demonstrated that mindfulness training can reduce the neural responses associated with cognitive conflict, thereby easing the psychological burden of dissonance.

If we foster a greater degree of emotional balance and cognitive flexibility, mindfulness can help us face challenges with increased resilience and help us to hold a more compassionate view of ourselves.

8.5.4 Getting Better, Not Bitter

Carol Dweck's research on mindsets provides important insights into how we, as humans, deal with cognitive dissonance related to personal failure.

It is important to remember that a fixed mindset, the belief that abilities are static and unchangeable, exacerbates the detrimental effects of dissonance because failures are seen as definitive of one's identity. In contrast, a growth mindset, the belief that abilities can be developed through effort and learning, allows individuals to view setbacks as opportunities for improvement.

Approaches aimed at fostering a growth mindset have been effective in academic and professional settings. Students who are taught to view intelligence as malleable are more likely to persevere in the face of challenging tasks and less likely to experience a drop in self-esteem after a poor performance.

If we promote the idea that failure is a natural and even necessary component of growth, a growth mindset approach helps reduce the severity of inner conflict and supports a more adaptive self-concept.

8.5.5 Build Don't Break

Given that social comparisons and external evaluations contribute significantly to cognitive dissonance, enhancing social support can be an effective strategy for buffering its effects.

Constructive feedback from trusted peers, mentors, and supervisors not only provides realistic perspectives on performance but also reinforces a broader and more balanced self-image.

Social support networks serve as a reality check, helping us to contextualise isolated failures within a larger framework of strengths and achievements.

Group-based approaches, such as peer support groups or collaborative workshops, can also provide safe spaces for us to share experiences, confront dissonance collectively, and learn adaptive coping strategies.
It has been shown that people who feel socially supported are less likely to internalise any harsh feedback and so avoid experiencing the full brunt of cognitive dissonance (Davis & Roberts, 2021).

8.6. From Theory to Practice
8.6.1 The Hidden Toll of Inner Conflict

When inner conflict remains unaddressed, its negative effects can become chronic. Persistent discrepancies between self-image and reality contribute to a host of adverse outcomes, including diminished self-esteem and increased anxiety.

In the longer term, unresolved conflict can reinforce harmful behaviour, reduce motivation, and impair relationships.

Looking forward, understanding cognitive dissonance's long-term effects is vital for clinical practice, as well as for education and organisational policy.

8.6.2 Who Shapes How We See Ourselves

Cultural narratives play a significant role in shaping self-image and the parameters by which we judge our own success or failure.

In societies that place heavy emphasis on achievement and perfection, the gap between the ideal self and the actual self may be especially pronounced, thereby increasing the likelihood and intensity of cognitive dissonance. Recognising these cultural factors is essential for tailoring treatments that respect and address the diverse ways in which self-worth is constructed around the world.

8.6.3 Looking Ahead

We should keep exploring the gap between self-image and reality, especially how dissonance changes over time and how early failures shape the way we see ourselves later in life.

This will help us to better understand how our self-esteem declines over time.

8.7 Harmonising Self-Image and Reality
8.7.1 Early Recognition

A critical step in mitigating the impact of cognitive dissonance is early recognition. We must become attuned to when our self-image is at odds with our real life. This can be done by spotting early warning signs, like, feelings of ongoing insecurity, constant self-doubt or being over critical of oneself.

8.7.2 Bridging the Gap

When all is said and done, the goal is not to eliminate cognitive dissonance entirely, which would be an unrealistic objective, given that life inherently presents both successes and failures, but to reconcile the differences in a way that supports personal growth.

This reconciliation involves both internal cognitive shifts and external behavioural adjustments. If we embrace a growth mindset, practicing self-compassion, and engaging in adaptive coping strategies, we can begin to accept that imperfections and setbacks are not reflections of our inherent worth but opportunities for evolution.

8.7.3 Building Resilience

One of the most effective ways to reduce the effects of cognitive dissonance is to develop a self-concept that is multifaceted rather than narrowly defined by any single domain of achievement. When self-esteem is built on a foundation of diverse strengths and values, a setback in one area does not threaten the entirety of our identity.

Educational, clinical, and organisational approaches can all contribute to building such resilience, fostering a robust, flexible self-image that is better equipped to absorb the inevitable discrepancies between ideal and actual performance.

8.7.4 Supportive Environments

In addition to personal strategies, supportive environments play a crucial role in mitigating cognitive dissonance.

Whether in schools, workplaces, or social communities, environments that emphasise growth, provide constructive feedback, and celebrate effort as much as outcome help us maintain a more balanced self-view.

Such environments not only reduce the intensity of dissonance but also provide the social scaffolding necessary for us to integrate challenging experiences into a positive self-narrative.

Conclusion

Cognitive dissonance is a powerful force in human psychology, one that arises when the image we hold of ourselves collides with the often more complicated reality of our experiences. This conflict, though common, can generate profound discomfort that affects our emotions, our decision-making, and our overall sense of worth.

When our inner structure begins to wobble, we often make it worse by looking sideways. We measure and compare ourselves to those who appear to be calmer, more competent, more confident.

Their life appears easier, simpler.

In this fragile moment when our own identity is under strain, comparison tightens the screws. The crack doesn't just widen; it reshapes the whole foundation. Bang!

As we measure ourselves against others, our frustration shifts from private discomfort to corrosive self-judgment.

Over the years, research, from Festinger's pioneering work in the 1950s to contemporary neuroscientific studies, has deepened our understanding of how dissonance emerges and the various strategies we, as human beings, can use to resolve it.

This chapter has explored where inner conflict comes from, especially when who we think we are clashes with what we experience in real life.
It has covered key ideas that explain this tension, how the brain responds to it, and everyday examples showing how it plays out. When these conflicts go unresolved, they can slowly wear down self-esteem and hold back our personal growth.

We have also discussed practical ways to handle the discomfort we feel, including cognitive-behavioural strategies, self-affirmation, mindfulness, and the benefits of developing a growth mindset.

Learning to spot inner conflict early, staying flexible in how we see ourselves and having a support network can make these challenges easier to manage.Eventually, the battle between self-image and reality need not be a source of perpetual distress; with the right strategies and support systems in place, it can become a catalyst for growth, deeper understanding of oneself, and enhanced well-being.

-9-

The Comparison Trap

Introduction

Social comparison does not create the gap between who we want to be and how we're actually doing, it magnifies it! In a world where our lives are constantly on display, it's hard not to compare ourselves to others. Social comparison shapes how we see ourselves, what drives us, and how we feel.

While comparison can sometimes motivate us, it often widens the gap between who we want to be and how we're actually doing, and that gap is where frustration grows.

Let's start to explore the multifaceted phenomenon of social comparison and how peer evaluation can fuel frustration. We will begin by introducing the theories that explain why and how we compare ourselves, then delve into cognitive and neurobiological mechanisms underlying the process. The discussion will cover how upward and downward comparisons affect self-esteem, the role of social media and group dynamics in intensifying these effects, and how persistent exposure to idealised images of success can lead to chronic frustration.

Throwing in some scenarios based on academic, workplace and personal relationships, we will illustrate the significant emotional toll that unfavourable comparisons can exert on us as individuals.

Finally, we will present strategies for mitigating the adverse effects of social comparisons. It is important to foster resilience and nurture a balanced self-image in settings where social comparison is pervasive.

9.1 How Social Comparison Shapes Us
9.1.1 Social Comparison Theory

Social comparison shapes how we see ourselves. When success is visible, comparing ourselves to others can quickly trigger feelings of inadequacy. As Festinger (1954) showed, we naturally use others as a benchmark, especially when clear standards are missing, and we tend to compare ourselves to people like us, which makes it hit harder.

This process is automatic. When we feel we're falling short, frustration or envy follows. Sometimes it motivates us, but when the gap feels too wide, it usually leads to frustration.

9.1.2 Extensions and Developments

Since Festinger's original theory, research has shown that social comparison isn't just about who we compare ourselves to, but what we compare, how often we do it, and how much it stands out in daily life (Suls et al., 2002).

These factors shape how strongly comparison affects us.

Self-discrepancy theory (Higgins, 1987) adds another layer: when there's a gap between who we are and who we want to be, our mood drops. When we compare ourselves to people who reflect that ideal, the gap feels sharper, intensifying feelings of inadequacy and frustration.

9.1.3 Upward and Downward Comparisons

Social comparison is not one way, we look up and we look down. Compare up, and you might feel inspired, or completely outclassed. Compare down, and you might feel better, but not for long.

Upward comparisons can motivate, but if the gap feels too big, they just leave you frustrated.

Downward comparisons give a quick confidence boost but become too dependent on those boosters and you stop pushing yourself.

In short: compare up and you either level up or feel deflated; compare down and you feel good, but risk getting a little too comfortable.

9.2 The Power of Expectation
9.2.1 Setting Ourselves Up for a Fall

Our unhappiness is not caused by the difficulties life throws at us from time to time, but how we define what is "normal". Somewhere on our journey into adulthood, we absorbed an airbrushed version of our grown-up life. In this version, normal people love their jobs, feel wildly compatible with their partners, wake up energised, regulate their emotions like clockwork, and never lie awake in the middle of the night wondering if they've made a terrible mistake.

In adult life we should be, calm, successful and sorted.

What's the problem?

The problem is that this is not the norm, it is very rare. Most people feel unsure about work. Most relationships include boredom, irritation, and phases of emotional static. Most of us compare, envy, overthink, and have the occasional suspicion that we're fundamentally flawed.

That's not dysfunction. That's called being human.

The real damage begins when we assume our struggles are unique. When we think, "Everyone else is fine, why am I the only one failing?"

That little voice in the back of our minds, doesn't just lead to sadness, it mutates into shame.

The inner commentary kicks in.

One mistake becomes, "Maybe I'm not good enough." A disagreement turns into, "Maybe this relationship was doomed from the start." Career doubt spirals into, "Maybe I'm not cut out for this." A landmark birthday arrives, goals unmet, and suddenly it's, "Maybe I've ruined my life."

It's never just the event. It's the story we attach to it.

Normal relationships come with friction. Normal careers come with doubt. Normal minds come with anxiety. Moreover, being a grown up? That includes lots of emotional homework.

When you accept that, something relaxes, there is a release and the pressure eases. You stop treating every wobble as a catastrophe. You stop interpreting discomfort as proof you're defective. You are not defective!

This isn't about lowering the bar. It's about ditching the fantasy. Realism, oddly enough, is comforting, because if struggle is standard, then you're not broken, you are participating, you are living.

A good life isn't a constant high. It's uneven, imperfect, occasionally dull, sometimes stressful but always extremely worthwhile.

9.2.2 The Myth of Normal

Comparison is not a modern invention, but it has become a modern obsession. It helps us to find our place within a group, calibrate our performance, and learn from those who excel.

The difficulty arises when comparison shifts from information-gathering to identity-evaluating. What begins as "How am I doing?" quickly becomes "Am I good enough?" Upward comparison, measuring ourselves against those we perceive as more successful, attractive, capable, or fulfilled can be particularly potent.

It has been consistently proved that while upward comparison can motivate improvement, it also increases dissatisfaction and self-criticism when the perceived gap feels unbridgeable.

In environments saturated with curated success, particularly through online platforms where achievements are selectively displayed, we are rarely comparing our ordinary Tuesday to someone else's ordinary Tuesday.

We are comparing our behind-the-scenes to their carefully edited reel.

The psychological cost of this constant measurement is subtle but cumulative. Repeated exposure to these polished standards alters our internal benchmark of "normal."

Over time, the extraordinary begins to feel standard, and our perfectly human fluctuations begin to feel like failures. The mind, already vulnerable to self-doubt, interprets difference as deficiency. In this way, comparison does not merely reflect insecurity; it actively amplifies it, magnifying the internal narrative that we are falling short.

9.3 The Thinking Behind Comparison
9.3.1 Sizing Ourselves Up

At its core, social comparison is a cognitive process of self-evaluation. When we compare, we are not simply observing others; we are actively retrieving, processing, and integrating information about who we believe ourselves to be in relation to them. The mind does not do this neutrally. It filters. It selects. It interprets.

We are particularly prone to confirmation bias, the tendency to notice and remember information that supports our existing self-view. If we already harbour doubts about our worth or competence, we will scan the environment for evidence that confirms it. We will notice their promotion, their engagement, their effortless confidence and quietly discount our own progress. In doing so, comparison stops helping us to grow and instead becomes a mechanism for reinforcing insecurity and deepening our feelings of inadequacy.

9.3.2 Why We Credit Ourselves or Don't

Attribution theory plays an important role in how we interpret our comparative standing, in other words, how we explain failure shapes how bad comparisons feel. When we fall short or feel less capable than others, we often blame ourselves in a profound and rigid way. An example of this would be a student who keeps getting lower grades than classmates, this may lead the student to decide they're just "not smart," instead of considering other factors like insufficient preparation or external distractions.

This attributional bias deepens the psychological impact of unfavourable comparisons, fuelling frustration and lowering self-esteem.

9.4 Hardwired to Compare
9.4.1 The Brain's Inner Scorecard

Brain scans show that social comparison lights up the same areas we use to think about ourselves and spot problems.

The medial prefrontal cortex (mPFC) builds our self-image, while the anterior cingulate cortex (ACC) is the internal alarm, going off when comparisons don't match how we see ourselves.

In simple terms: one part of our brain writes our story while the other part panics when someone else's story looks better.

9.4.2 Emotional Responses

Brain chemistry gets involved too. Dopamine gives us a positive energy boost when comparing ourselves to others and it gives us the sensation we might even catch up.

Yet if the gap feels too wide, that boost disappears and frustration or envy kicks in. Serotonin helps to keep us steady, but when it is low, we have less patience and reactions get more extreme.

Instead of dealing with it rationally, we might snap just to feel better and let off some steam.

9.4.3 Stress & Social Evaluation

As discussed earlier, the brain's stress system is highly sensitive to social evaluation. Repeated adverse comparisons can keep the system switched on, and that alarm just won't stop ringing!

Cortisol stays high, thinking gets foggy, patience runs thin, and your mood goes down, big time!.

The result?

You feel worse, compare more, and stay stuck in a counterproductive loop.

9.5 Putting Social Comparison in Context
9.5.1 The World of Academia

In academic settings, comparison is basically a full-time job. Students constantly measure themselves against each other. High achievers stress over tiny drops in grades; others feel like they're permanently behind. Either way, it fuels anxiety and chips away at confidence.

Focus should be on learning, not ranking. That way it's a lot less painful.

9.5.2 Performing at Work

At work, comparison never clocks out. You're measured and checked out against colleagues in reviews, meetings, even casual chats. Fall behind, and frustration, resentment, and job dissatisfaction creep in fast.

Picture a hardworking manager continually compared to the office star, maybe jokingly or through formal feedback. Their confidence dips, motivation slips, and burnout won't be far behind. Businesses that focus on collaboration instead of competition work better!

9.5.3 How We Love & Relate

In relationships, comparison is the fast track to frustration. We measure our partners and our lives against other people's highlights and suddenly nothing feels good enough. When these comparisons highlight perceived deficiencies, the resulting frustration can lead to conflict and dissatisfaction. Families aren't much better, siblings compare, rivalries grow, and someone always feels like the 'less successful' one.

Drop the comparisons, and life becomes a lot more fun!

9.6 Comparison is the Thief of Contentment
9.6.1 Worn Down from Within

Constant comparison is like slowly letting the air out of your own confidence balloon. The more you see others doing better, the bigger the gap feels, and the worse you feel. Continue long enough and you end up anxious and depressed, with that inner voice becoming a very harsh and annoying coach. A little comparison motivates but too much is unhealthy.

Get a grip and don't end up being your own worst critic!

9.6.2 Withdrawal and Aggression

Too much comparison doesn't just feel bad; it makes people act weird. Some withdraw and avoid situations where they might be judged. Others go on the attack, snapping at colleagues or even bullying others to make themselves feel better. Either way, it wrecks relationships and keeps the cycle going: feel worse, act worse, repeat.

Break the cycle!

9.6.3 Impact on Mental Health

Persistent social comparison isn't just draining, it's damaging. Over time, it's linked to anxiety, depression, and even eating disorders, especially when appearance is the focus. Teenagers who constantly compare themselves upward are more likely to develop depression later in life (Higgins, 1987).

We are all different with different capabilities and talents. It is good to compare ourselves to others in small doses and for the right reasons, it can motivate us to improve, learn from others, and set clearer, more realistic goals. It can also inspire ambition, boost confidence, and help us understand where we stand while feeling connected to those around us.

Comparison is not the problem; it is how you use it!

9.8 Moving Forward
9.8.1 Building Resilience

One of the best ways to soften the adverse effects of social comparison is to build a strong, well-rounded sense of self.

When we don't tie our worth to just one aspect of ourselves, like performance, looks, or approval we are less shaken when unfavourable comparisons occur.

If we can spot unhealthy comparison habits early, it is easier to seek remedy before things spiral out of control.

Conclusion

Social comparison is part of being human, but left to roam, it can quietly destroy your confidence. When the gap between you and your 'ideal' feels too big, frustration, poor self-esteem, and even depression sets in.

The good news?

You don't need to stop comparing, just manage it better.

With the right mindset and support, comparison can push you forward instead of pulling you apart.

-10-
When Good Intentions Go Wrong

Introduction

Aggression can be useful when it's controlled, such as when we need to defend our boundaries or compete.

Trouble starts when frustration and misplaced emotions drive aggression in the wrong direction. Instead of addressing the real problem, anger gets taken out on easier targets, harming others, possibly also the aggressor and the wider community.

This happens across daily life online and offline.

When confronting the true source of stress feels risky or impossible, we may displace our anger onto a less powerful, less threatening target. While this may offer brief relief, it usually causes damage far greater than the original trigger.

As before, this chapter uses scenarios to show how misguided aggression develops, the mental and neural processes behind it, and the social situations that fuel it, before concluding with approaches to reduce misdirected anger and prevent unintended harm.

10.1 When Anger Goes Sideways

When we can't aim our anger at the real problem, we aim it somewhere safer. In other words, when the boss is off-limits, the coffee machine, or a colleague, gets a bashing instead, figuratively speaking of course.

10.1.1 Keeping Score

Social comparison can also stir the pot. When people stack themselves against others and feel they fall short, the disconnect between who they are and who they want to be can generate exasperation.

That tension needs somewhere to go, unfortunately, it can end up directed at the nearest innocent bystander.

10.2 Anger Misfired
10.2.1 Mind Tricks & Misplaced Blame

The mind loves a shortcut. One mistake becomes "I'm useless," and suddenly someone else is to blame. It's a convenient way to patch up a bruised ego, but the damage is outsourced to mended.

10.2.2 Brain Mechanics of Aggression

As we are now fully aware, when reality clashes with how we see ourselves, the brain sounds the alarm. Emotions ramp up and self-control jumps out the window.

Remember a stressed brain equals a shorter fuse.

10.2.3 Environmental and Social Stressors

External pressure, competition, and a bit of judgment can build frustration fast. In environments where there is a high degree of evaluation or where performance is constantly compared against ideal standards, we, as human beings, are more likely to experience frustration.

The availability of vulnerable targets, whether due to power differentials or social hierarchies, further increases the risk of displaced aggression, which can lead to unintended harm.

10.3 The "Scapegoat" Phenomenon

Below are some scenarios to illustrate the diverse settings and manifestations of misguided aggression. These snapshots provide insight into the processes by which frustration becomes misdirected, as well as the consequent harm inflicted upon targets who are often not at all responsible for the original stress.

10.3.1 In the Workplace

Overview

Consider the case of a middle manager in a competitive corporate environment. This staff member faced mounting pressure due to an aggressive sales target imposed by senior management. Unable to confront the high-stakes expectations directly and frustrated by bureaucratic obstacles beyond his control, the manager began to displace his growing anger onto a subordinate perceived to be less powerful.

Dynamics and Consequences

The subordinate was repeatedly blamed for minor mistakes and criticised in public meetings. Over time, the performance and confidence of the subordinate declined, leading to emotional distress, increased absence and eventual resignation. While the manager felt brief relief, unresolved stress later spread across the team, reducing morale and productivity.

This case shows how workplace pressure and rigid hierarchies can encourage scapegoating of vulnerable employees.

Research by Davis and Roberts (2021) supports the link between high-pressure environments and limited outlets leading to a higher number of confrontations.

10.3.2 In the Home

Overview

In another context, consider a family where one parent works in a high-pressure corporate job with long hours and constant deadlines. The cumulative stress from professional life begins to take an emotional toll.

Instead of addressing the root causes of their stress, such as workplace conflicts or unrealistic expectations, the parent begins to unconsciously displace their frustration onto their children.

Dynamics and Consequences

Displaced aggression shows up as verbal outbursts, harsh discipline and emotional withdrawal, with children, often the most vulnerable, absorbing the impact.

Research links ongoing parental aggression to long-term effects such as anxiety, depression and difficulty forming healthy relationships.

This example highlights the importance of addressing stress at its source, as misdirected frustration can cause lasting harm to children.

10.3.3 Sports: Aggression on the Field
Overview

Competitive sports can foster misplaced aggression. After a key mistake in an important tournament, an elite athlete, under heavy public and personal pressure, experienced intense frustration.

Dynamics and Consequences

Unable to confront the pressures of competition, the athlete redirected anger toward a teammate during practice, disrupting team cohesion and damaging his public image. In sport, repeated outbursts don't just vent frustration, they can damage reputations and invite disciplinary action, revealing how thin the line is between fierce competition and losing control.

10.3.4 Collective Aggression and Scapegoating

Overview

On a larger scale, entire groups can engage in collective displacement. During periods of economic downturn, for instance, societal tensions often escalate, and political leaders or media figures may exploit these emotions by blaming a particular minority group for broader societal problems.

Dynamics and Consequences

During periods of rapid social change, economic frustration is often redirected toward immigrant communities, who become scapegoats for broader hardship.

While this may offer brief emotional relief, it leads to discrimination, violence, and lasting social division. Research by Smith et al. (2023) links collective displacement to higher societal stress, reinforcing cycles of scapegoating and retaliatory aggression.

10.3.5 Cyberbullying

Overview

The digital age has created new outlets for aggression, with cyberbullying emerging as a common form of misdirected anger.

For example, an adolescent experiencing social isolation may redirect frustration into online attacks against a more popular peer.

Dynamics and Consequences

Online anonymity reduces accountability, emboldening repeated hostility while exposing targets to public humiliation and emotional harm.

This case shows how digital platforms amplify misguided aggression, making it an urgent focus for new approaches and solutions.

10.4 Collateral Damage of Misguided Aggression
10.4.1 The Trauma & Distress

Victims of misguided aggression, wherever it occurs, often suffer from profound psychological trauma. Repeated exposure to unmerited hostility can lead to symptoms of post-traumatic stress disorder (PTSD), chronic anxiety, and depression.

The emotional scars left by such aggression undermine a person's ability to trust others and to feel secure within their own environment.

10.4.2 The Social Consequences

Beyond individual harm, misguided aggression can erode the fabric of interpersonal relationships and community cohesion. In the workplace, for example, persistent scapegoating can create a climate of fear and mistrust, undermining collaboration and productivity. At the societal level, collective scapegoating can polarise communities, fostering an environment of discrimination and conflict that is difficult to heal.

10.4.3 The Long Shadow Cast

The unintended harm of misguided aggression is not confined to isolated incidents; its long-term repercussions often manifest as broken systems and institutional breakdowns.In families, cycles of aggression can be intergenerational, with children learning pathological behaviours that perpetuate emotional dysfunction. In societies, the cumulative effect of collective displacement can lead to entrenched social inequalities and persistent tensions within communities.

10.5 What Happens Next
10.5.1 More to Explore

Misguided anger is a shared community challenge that spans multiple areas of our daily lives. No single service can address it alone. Community organisations are uniquely positioned to bring together educators, youth workers, mental health providers and local leaders to identify early signs of stress, reduce pressure and intervene before frustration turns into destructive behaviour.

Through coordinated prevention efforts, shared resources and evidence-based programmes, communities can build emotional regulation skills, create safe outlets for anger and support both young people and adults, helping to reduce aggression within communities, strengthen resilience and improve long-term social wellbeing for all members of society.

10.5.2 Cross-Cultural Perspectives

How people compare themselves to others and how anger gets expressed, depends heavily on culture and prevailing attitudes. Reviewing different cultural settings can help explain why misguided aggression shows up in different ways across communities. This kind of investigation can uncover culture-specific risks and protective factors, leading to new approaches that actually fit the social circumstances rather than applying one-size-fits-all solutions.

Conclusion

Misguided aggression, taking your anger out on the wrong person, shows up everywhere: at work, at home and social media. It's driven by dysfunctional reasoning and stress. Having a blow-out might feel great in the moment but the fallout is messy, it damages relationships, lowers confidence, and leaves a lot of regret. The fix isn't complicated, but it takes effort: spot it early, manage your reactions, and stop treating other people like emotional punchbags. The journey toward reducing the collateral damage of misguided aggression is challenging, but with continued effort and a commitment to fostering healthier interpersonal and societal dynamics, significant progress can be made. As we look to the future, a multidisciplinary and culturally sensitive approach will be vital in addressing this pervasive issue and ensuring that the energies of frustration are harnessed in ways that benefit rather than injure.

-11-

Fallout: When Anger Damages Relationships

Introduction

Relationships are at the heart of being human. They give us support, a sense of belonging and room to grow, both as individuals and as a society.

When conflict erupts, especially if driven by misdirected anger, built-up frustration, or poor emotional control, the damage rarely stays contained. Toxic behaviour spills beyond the moment, rippling through families, friendships, workplaces, and the wider community.

Relationships may suffer when individuals internalise conflicts, blame others or retreat from social interactions. The fallout is often not confined to a single interaction; rather, the consequences may accumulate over time, eroding trust, intimacy, and emotional stability.

In many cases, patterns of misdirected aggression and persistent frustration create cycles that lead to long-term relational dysfunction and even systemic issues within families, organisations and communities. Most relationship meltdowns do not start with one big moment, they unravel through small habits: snap judgments, inner contradictions, simmering stress, and the occasional emotional grenade.

If you have ever wondered how relationships go from fine to "how did we get here?" We will now dig into those patterns that start the slide and discuss some strategies on how to repair the damage and stop the pattern.

Pressure Cooker

11.1 Tension Takeover
11.1.1 The Invisible Rules of Connection

Attachment theory offers a clear lens for understanding relationship fallout. First articulated by Bowlby (1969) and expanded by Ainsworth and colleagues, the theory suggests that early relational experiences shape expectations in adult relationships.

Secure attachment is associated with trust, effective communication and adaptive conflict management, whereas insecure attachment styles such as being anxious, dismissive, emotionally distant and disorganised, are linked to greater difficulty during relational strain.

When aggressive or misdirected behaviour occurs, individuals with insecure attachment patterns are more likely to interpret it as rejection or abandonment, amplifying the emotional distress and threatening relationship stability (Johnson & Miller, 2021). These patterns often recur across adult relationships, reinforcing recurring dysfunctional patterns that contribute to the ripple effect of hostility.

11.1.2 The Cost–Benefit Side of Relationships

The cost–benefit side of relationships is captured by social exchange and equity theories, which frame everyday interactions in terms of costs, rewards, and fairness (Homans, 1958; Adams, 1965).

When contributions feel balanced, relationships tend to feel satisfying and stable.

In contrast, when one person repeatedly acts aggressively or stops giving back, that balance breaks down, disrupting the sense of fairness that keeps the relationship functioning.

Let's take the example of a coworker who habitually directs misplaced aggression at a teammate, the imbalance of the emotional cost may lead to feelings of resentment and disengagement. Gradually this inequity can result in reduced collaboration, diminished trust, and, ultimately, the erosion of the relationship. Several studies have revealed that perceived unfairness at work contributes to lower job satisfaction and increased staff turnover (Davis & Roberts, 2021).

11.1.3 The Relationship Ripple Effect

Family systems theory (Minuchin, 1974) views the family as a dynamic, interconnected system in which each member's behaviour affects the whole unit. When conflict arises, such as through misdirected aggression or unresolved frustration, the effects propagate throughout the family network, for instance, parental aggression may not only harm the immediate target but also influence sibling relationships and even the marital bond. Little by little, these ripple effects can foster patterns of poor communication, emotional distancing and even intergenerational cycles of toxic behaviour. Such systemic fallout can be especially damaging, as it disrupts the family's overall equilibrium and hampers each member's ability to develop healthy relationship skills for the future.

11.2 The Hidden Slide to Relationship Breakdown
11.2.1 When Our Reasoning Works Against Us

When our behaviour clashes with how we see ourselves, or when we feel that we have been treated unfairly, we experience cognitive dissonance, as discussed in chapter eight. This causes us much discomfort and so we try to resolve it by justifying our actions, rewriting the story in our heads, or shifting the blame onto someone or something else.

In relationships, this often appears as, what is known as, attribution errors: instead of looking at the situation objectively, we blame the other person's character, for instance, a missed appointment becomes proof that they are unreliable. Over time, this black-and-white thinking hardens the narrative. What may have started as a misunderstanding begins to feel like a betrayal. When we slip into these thinking traps, conflict feels like a personal attack, making relationship breakdown far more likely.

11.2.2 How Harsh Self-Judgement Makes Us Vulnerable

Deep-seated self-doubt or distorted views of ourselves, what is known as negative self-schemas, acts like a mental filter on our social lives. If we secretly believe we are not good enough, even neutral moments can start to feel like criticism or rejection. In relationships, this vulnerability can trigger defensive behaviours, like withdrawal or aggression, that further destabilise the connection.

Imagine a partner with a self-critical narrative, he or she, may react disproportionately to minor criticisms, perceiving them as confirmation of their worst fears. When there is repeated exposure, these defensive reactions can erode trust and intimacy. Studies indicate that individuals, with an entrenched self-critical narrative, have a heightened risk of falling into depression after a hostile confrontation.

11.2.3 Poor Emotional Control

Effective emotional regulation is central to managing any turbulence that happens within a relationship. Nevertheless, it is not always easy to control our emotions especially when we are under chronic stress or suffering from negative social comparisons or some other internal conflict.

These additional pressures can impair our ability to regulate our emotions, and this deficit often leads to impulsive behaviour, such as outbursts of anger or abrupt withdrawal, which then further strains the relationship.

When the prefrontal cortex is less active, people tend to be more aggressive and have higher relationship conflict. Those with compromised self-control may be unable to pause and reflect during a conflict, instead reacting in ways that are disproportionate to the situation. These patterns, if repeated over time, contribute to a cycle of escalating conflict.

11.3 The Chain Reaction
11.3.1 Familial Conflict

Overview

If we look at this through the lens of attachment and relationship systems, trouble often starts when roles blur and power is not equal. Children are particularly vulnerable because they rely on adults for emotional safety, consistency and fairness. When stress or fear of being judged disrupts that balance, relationships can easily become unhealthy.

Dynamics and Consequences

Consider a child who has an aunt and this aunt is also her teacher at school. If we consider this situation from an educational psychology standpoint, the aunt is operating under sustained professional pressure, managing classroom behaviour, academic outcomes and peer scrutiny, while also navigating the added complexity of teaching a family member. Concerned about accusations of favouritism, she becomes overly vigilant and rigid in her interactions with her niece.

Viewed through attachment theory, the aunt's heightened criticism and emotional withdrawal undermine the child's sense of security. Rather than experiencing the aunt as a reliable and supportive figure, the child begins to perceive unpredictability and rejection, particularly during moments of stress or correction. If a child starts to have emerging or insecure attachment patterns, this can intensify anxiety, self-doubt and confusion about what to expect from relationships. The systems theory perspective states that behaviour is maintained by the broader family. The aunt occupies a position of authority in both settings, while the parents, trusting her professional role, are unlikely to challenge her actions. This lack of corrective feedback creates a closed loop in which stress is displaced downward onto the child, who has the least power to resist or reframe the dynamic. Gradually, the child internalises these experiences, which may shape self-critical narrative patterns and expectations of unfair treatment in other relationships. The overlap of family, educational, and emotional systems allows the aunt's unresolved stress to ripple outward, producing relational strain that extends beyond the classroom and into the family unit. This scenario illustrates how a communication breakdown is not the result of a single interaction, but of repeated, unaddressed dynamics embedded within the relationship.

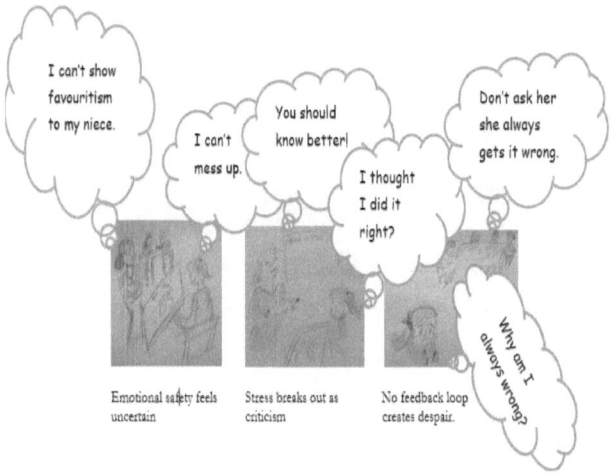

The Right Way

However, if the situation is handled well, the aunt recognises the pressure created by her dual role as both teacher and family member.

Worried about appearing biased, it's easy to overcorrect with extra strictness, but this course of action can leave the child feeling singled out rather than supported. A healthier approach is to keep expectations fair while maintaining warmth and patience.

When mistakes happen, the focus shifts from criticism to guidance: explaining the task, encouraging questions, and reminding the child that learning involves trial and error. If the aunt stays calm and transparent she will restore a sense of safety and predictability.

The child experiences correction as part of learning, not rejection, and the wider family and school system remain open to feedback rather than stuck in a silent, toxic loop.

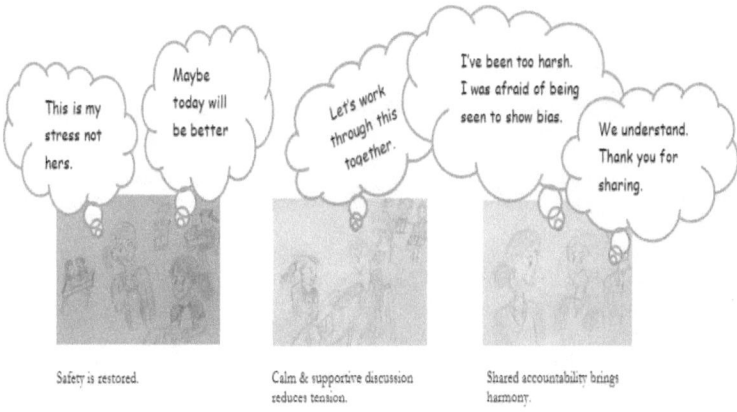

Safety is restored.

Calm & supportive discussion reduces tension.

Shared accountability brings harmony.

11.3.2 Strain at Work

Overview

Workplace relationships can become strained when pressure flows unevenly through organisational hierarchies. When senior leaders face external demands, such as investor scrutiny or performance expectations, stress is not always absorbed at the top. Instead, it may be redirected toward those in subordinate roles, setting the stage for relational strain and organisational dysfunction.

Dynamics and Consequences

A managing director is under sustained pressure from investors to deliver rapid financial returns. Shareholder meetings are tense; expectations are escalating and tolerance for uncertainty is shrinking. Within this context, the managing director begins to focus intensely on the financial director, whose role becomes the primary point of control and reassurance. Deadlines tighten, financial projections are scrutinised repeatedly, and conversations shift from collaborative problem-solving to interrogation.

When Pressure Flows Downwards

Unchecked stress cascades down, impacting rest of the team.

Narrow focus breeds tension and compliance.

Questions are framed with urgency and impatience, and minor discrepancies are treated as major concerns. In this dynamic, rather than absorbing the pressure, the managing director channels his anxiety toward the financial director. After a while, this redistribution of pressure alters the relationship. The financial director becomes cautious, defensive and risk-averse, while trust and open communication erode.

Rather than stabilising the organisation, the downward flow of stress amplifies dysfunction across the team.

The Right Way

In a contrasting scenario, the managing director recognises that investor pressure is destabilising internal relationships. Rather than intensifying control over the financial director, they pause and broaden the system response. Expectations are clarified, uncertainty is acknowledged and responsibility for managing external pressure is shared across the team.

Regular check-ins shift from fault-finding to joint planning. The managing director names the external constraints openly, invites feedback and resists the urge to contain anxiety by tightening oversight.

In this dynamic, pressure is absorbed and redistributed horizontally rather than pushed downward. As a result, trust stabilises, communication becomes more transparent and the leadership system regains flexibility. The relationship between managing director and financial director shifts back toward collaboration, illustrating how conscious regulation at the top of the system can prevent relational fallout and strengthen productivity and collaboration.

Repairing the System

Team motivated and stability restored.

Flexible & supportive leadership supports strategic growth.

11.3.3 Connected, Yet Apart: The Digital Age

Overview

Online criticism affects everyone, but it hits teenagers much harder. When identity is still forming, harsh or hostile feedback can quickly shape how young people see themselves and how they relate to others.

Without support to buffer these experiences, online conflict can spill beyond the screen, creating a chain reaction that impacts their behaviour, confidence and relationships.

Dynamics and Consequences

While adults often have more stable identities and coping strategies to fall back on, adolescents are still forming their sense of self and learning how to manage emotional setbacks. For a teenager, feedback, especially public feedback, can feel deeply personal.

Consider a teenage girl who starts a travel blog to share family holidays and personal adventures. At first, the experience is exciting and affirming. Posting photos from the beach or writing about new places brings positive comments and engagement, which boosts her confidence and sense of belonging.

This is in line with Valkenburg et al. (2006), who confirmed that online affirmation can temporarily strengthen self-esteem and social connection for young people Sadly, as time passes, the tone of the responses start to change. Anonymous users leave critical remarks about her appearance, body shape, or clothing. While an adult might dismiss these comments as rude or meaningless, a teenager is more likely to take them to heart.

Viewed through an attachment lens, repeated criticism is experienced less as opinion and more as rejection, threatening a young person's sense of acceptance and emotional safety (Bowlby, 1969; Mikulincer & Shaver, 2007). Without fully developed coping skills, she begins to internalise the comments, slowly weaving them into how she sees herself (Harter, 2012).

As the feedback continues, her thinking and emotional responses shift. She checks comments repeatedly, goes over hurtful remarks and edits or deletes posts to avoid further judgment.

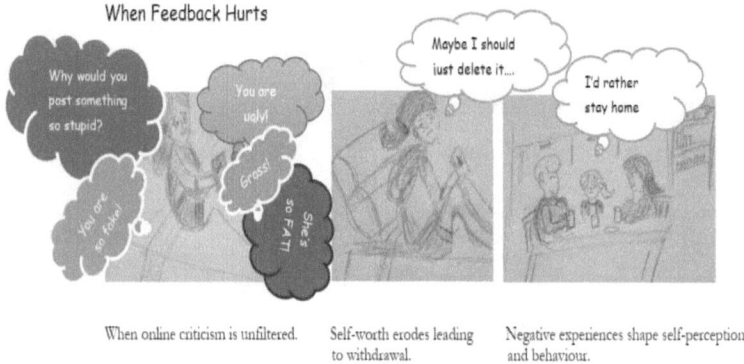

When online criticism is unfiltered.   Self-worth erodes leading   Negative experiences shape self-perception
                                         to withdrawal.   and behaviour.

These patterns reflect difficulties in emotional regulation, something that even adults can struggle with, but which is still developing during adolescence (Gross, J., 2015). Eventually, she starts to withdraw. She posts less, shares less with friends and becomes more socially cautious. What once made her feel creative and empowered now makes her feel exposed and unsafe.

Seen within the wider setting, this withdrawal can easily go unnoticed. Family members may interpret her behaviour as normal teenage moodiness rather than a response to persistent online abuse.

In the absence of adult guidance or peer support to help put the criticism into context, the online environment becomes a closed loop in which cruel messages carry more weight than positive ones (Minuchin, 1974).

As time passes, this can solidify a self-critical narrative and increase sensitivity to rejection, patterns that may later shape adult relationships, conflict responses and self-worth (Downey & Feldman, 1996).

This scenario highlights how fallout rarely comes from a single comment. Instead, it builds gradually through repeated, unbuffered interactions. While adults are not immune to these effects, teenagers are particularly vulnerable because their identities, emotional regulation skills and relational expectations are still taking shape.

How the Situation Should Be Managed

The teenager's distress should not remain invisible. As soon as a parent or caregiver notices changes in her behaviour, like withdrawal, irritability, reluctance to post or talk about her blog, they should gently invite her to a conversation.

When the teenager shares the harsh and undeserved comments she has received, the caregiver responds with validation rather than minimisation, acknowledging the hurt and unfairness of the criticism.

Looking at this scenario from an attachment perspective, this response restores emotional safety by communicating that the teenager is not alone in managing social rejection.

The parent or caregiver helps externalise the comments, framing them as reflections of online culture rather than truths about the teenager's worth or appearance. Practical steps are taken together, such as moderating comments, limiting exposure or reframing the purpose of the blog.

Peers can also play a protective role. Friends offer reassurance, challenge the negative narratives and reinforce a sense of belonging offline. Supportive voices open space for feedback, interrupting the cycle of internalised criticism.

Stress is shared and buffered rather than absorbed in isolation. Over time, the teenager regains confidence, re-engages with her interests and develops more resilient strategies for navigating online feedback.

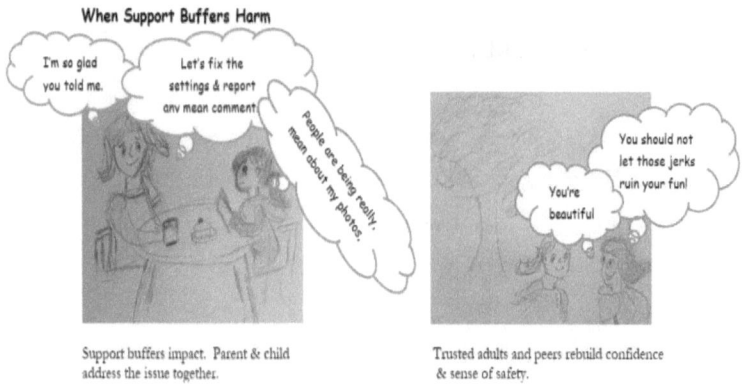

Support buffers impact. Parent & child address the issue together.

Trusted adults and peers rebuild confidence & sense of safety.

11.3.4 When Conflict Hijacks Connection

Overview

In intimate relationships, unresolved conflict and misplaced frustration can do a surprising amount of damage, especially when everyday responsibilities start to look less like teamwork and more like a solo project. Take a couple living together where both partners work, but the running of the household somehow ends up on one person's unofficial job description. The girlfriend cleans, does the dishes, and keeps the place functioning, usually after finishing her own workday, but like good Wi-Fi, her effort is mostly invisible until it stops working. Meanwhile, the boyfriend is busy too. He works long hours and, when he's off the clock, makes sure to recharge with friends. He feels that his life is already packed to the brim with responsibility and obligation.

On the other hand, she feels that the imbalance is becoming impossible to ignore. Left unaddressed, what started as a simple misallocation of household chores, slowly becomes a relationship crisis, one that quietly breeds resentment and begins to place distance between them.

Dynamics and Consequences

The girlfriend makes several attempts to address the imbalance. At first, she raises the issue carefully, suggesting they talk about sharing household chores more evenly. She explains that she is tired and that managing both work and domestic responsibilities feels overwhelming.

Rather than engaging in the conversation, the boyfriend avoids it. His responses are brief and deflective: *"I don't have time to talk about this right now,"* or *"You have to accept that I need to go out with my friends."* The discussion is repeatedly postponed or shut down before it begins.

This avoidance may not stem from indifference alone. The boyfriend may feel ill-equipped to navigate conversations about fairness, responsibility or emotional needs. Confronted with discomfort or perceived criticism, he disengages, choosing distance over dialogue.

The impact of this continued pattern on the relationship takes its toll, with each dismissed attempt leaving the girlfriend feeling increasingly unheard and undervalued.

As resentment mounts, her efforts to communicate become tinged with frustration. In response, the boyfriend grows more defensive, reinforcing a cycle in which one partner pursues resolution while the other withdraws. In the end, emotional connection erodes.

The girlfriend may begin to pull back emotionally, no longer raising concerns because past attempts have felt futile. The boyfriend, in turn, may interpret this withdrawal as acceptance or indifference, further widening the gap between them. In close relationships, like this one, unresolved conflict, avoidance and negative attribution patterns can significantly increase the risk of long-term dissatisfaction and separation (Rosenberg, 1965).

When everyday frustrations are repeatedly deflected rather than addressed, anger and resentment are displaced into the relationship itself. Both partners are left vulnerable to a gradual erosion of trust, mutual respect and emotional intimacy.

Conflict & Avoidance

I don't have time for this now.

You must understand; I need to go out with my friends!

Deflection of difficult topics causes relationship harm & distance.

She feels undervalued as he withdraws.

The Right Way

To avoid the breakdown of this relationship, the pattern of avoidance is interrupted before resentment fully hardens. After another tense evening marked by silence and unfinished dishes, the girlfriend chooses a different moment to speak, one that is calmer and not immediately tied to frustration. Rather than focusing solely on chores, she explains how the imbalance makes her feel: tired, unappreciated and increasingly disconnected.

This time, the boyfriend does not deflect. Although visibly uncomfortable, he stays in the conversation. If we consider this from an attachment perspective, his earlier avoidance can be understood as a protective strategy, an attempt to manage discomfort, perceived criticism or fear of inadequacy by shutting down emotionally.

Despite this, he remains present rather than disengaging, he begins to tolerate the tension that has built up in the relationship instead of trying to escape from it.

He acknowledges that when the topic of chores comes up, he feels overwhelmed and unsure how to respond. Avoiding the conversation had felt easier than risking conflict or failure.

Acknowledging this pattern allows both partners to see the issue not as a personal flaw but more as a shared challenge.

Engagement & Repair: Finding a Solution Together

I didn't realise how you felt.

Let's figure this out together.

Now we have a dishwasher, no more arguing over who does the dishes!

I love you

I love you.

He shares his feelings & she listens without criticism. This brings closeness. In this way they work together to find a solution.

They address the conflict together. Creatively and patiently they find a solution.

Solution found, harmony & balance restored. Happy days ahead!

Rather than continuing to argue over fairness in the moment, they shift toward problem-solving together.

They recognise that the repeated conflict around dishes has become symbolic, less about plates and more about feeling supported. As a practical step, they decide to buy a dishwasher. The choice is not about avoiding responsibility, but about reducing a recurring pressure point that has been fuelling resentment. This solution represents a broader shift in the relationship. Instead of one partner pursuing and the other avoiding, they collaborate.

The dishwasher becomes a tangible expression of shared responsibility and mutual care, allowing both partners to step out of the conflict cycle. As they address the avoidance, regulate emotional responses and introduce a practical buffer, the couple restores a sense of partnership and emotional safety.

In this way, repair does not come from perfectly equal chore distribution, but from engagement instead of avoidance and from recognising that unresolved, everyday conflicts, if ignored, can quietly undermine intimacy, while small, shared decisions can help restore it.

11.4 When Pain Snowballs
11.4.1 Disruption of Social Cohesion

When social fallout becomes widespread, its effects are felt far beyond immediate relationships. Cycles of misdirected aggression and unresolved conflict undermine social cohesion.

Communities may become polarised, with subgroups mistrusting each other due to recurring patterns of blame, retaliation, and exclusion. Such environments are less conducive to collective problem-solving and are at greater risk for systemic issues such as absentee leadership, reduced civic engagement and social fragmentation.

11.4.2 The Legacy of Conflict

Conflict rarely starts for no reason. In many families, it is passed down. Children who grow up around hate, misdirected anger and unresolved conflict often absorb these patterns, carrying them into their own adult relationships without even realising it. Over time, the cycle repeats itself, fuelling low self-esteem, poor emotional regulation and strained relationships. What may begin as a private relationship breakdown does not stay contained. Gradually, it spills outward, shaping families, workplaces and even the well-being of entire communities.

11.4.3 Economic Consequences

The fallout resulting from misguided aggression can also have significant economic and organisational consequences. In business settings, chronic conflict, mistrust, and deteriorating teamwork can lead to decreased productivity, increased employee turnover and diminished profitability.

Moreover, the broader impact of workplace aggression can extend to a loss of organisational reputation, making it more difficult to attract and retain talent. Davis and Roberts proved in 2021 that entities with hostile climates experience higher rates of burnout, absenteeism and reduced overall performance.

11.5 Repairing Relationship Fallout
11.5.1 Conflict Resolution

A proactive approach to minimising fallout involves structured conflict resolution strategies and mediation. Trained mediators can facilitate discussions between conflicting parties, helping them to communicate their feelings and perspectives in a controlled, neutral environment.

People are guided to acknowledge their own contributions to the conflict and to develop mutual solutions, mediation can break the cycle of blame and retaliation.

Evidence suggests that organisations and families that invest in conflict resolution training observe improved communication, enhanced trust and a reduction in recurring disputes.

11.5.2 Organisational and Policy-Level

On a broader scale, organisations, schools and communities can adopt policies that foster a culture of openness, collaboration, and mutual respect.

Implementing clear guidelines for conflict resolution, incentivising teamwork and providing regular opportunities for feedback can help create an environment where miscommunication and aggression are minimised.

Additionally, policies that emphasise work-life balance and stress management not only improve individual well-being but also reduce the probability that conflicts will lead to dysfunctional relationship patterns.

11.5.3 Communication in the Digital World

With the increasing prevalence of digital communication, it is imperative to examine how virtual interactions contribute to or mitigate relationship fallout.
Studies into the unique challenges of online conflict, including the anonymity, permanence and amplification effects of social media, are crucial.

11.5.4 Cultural Considerations

Culture significantly shapes how individuals engage in social comparison and conflict resolution. Cross-cultural studies can illuminate how different societies manage interpersonal fallout, and what protective factors might buffer against destructive patterns of aggression. Tailoring approaches to respect cultural differences will be essential in promoting global well-being and fostering healthy relationships across diverse communities.

Conclusion

Relationship breakdown rarely arrives with a dramatic bang. More often, it creeps in through unresolved conflict, misdirected frustration, and the slow build-up of everyday stress. Left unchecked, these patterns can quietly damage the relationships that hold our lives together.

We have discussed how aggression, distorted thinking, and poor emotional regulation can combine to push relationships off course. The fallout does not end with the couple, family, or colleagues involved. Research shows that unresolved conflict can erode self-esteem, fuel anxiety, weaken trust, and even ripple into workplaces and communities. In other words, relationship drama rarely stays contained.

The good news?

Humans are remarkably good at repairing things when they know what to look for. Practices like cognitive-behavioural strategies, mindfulness, better communication skills, and thoughtful workplace policies can all help reset the dynamic.

Pressure Cooker

Ultimately, repairing relationship breakdown is not about winning arguments, it's about understanding the mix of thoughts, emotions, and social pressures driving the conflict in the first place. With earlier awareness, better problem-solving, and stronger support networks, conflicts can shift from destructive spirals into opportunities for growth.

Fixing relationships is not easy, period. That said, given how much our well-being depends on them, few things are more worthwhile repairing.

-12-

Riding Out Emotional Storms

Introduction

You wake up with the day's agenda churning in your brain, that trip, that project, that parent-teacher meeting, that deadline you can't afford to miss. Your phone is already buzzing with messages before breakfast and by mid-morning you're juggling other people's expectations, and a growing list of things you'd forgotten the day before!

Does your brain ever feel like "an internet browser with twenty-one tabs open, six of which are frozen and you have no idea where the music is coming from?" Welcome to the club!

Modern life is chaotic and it seems to be becoming ever more so! Work, relationships, health! Infinite notifications!

Something is always competing for our attention and draining our emotional batteries. No wonder the mind occasionally feels like it's caught in an electrical storm or about to crash, like our internet browser.

The good news is that we're not completely helpless or hopeless. There are remedies at hand, like mindfulness, meditation and self-regulation. These techniques will not always stop us from being blown off course, but they can help us to stay afloat.

Firstly, we'll explore mindfulness, an idea that began in ancient times but is now backed by modern science. Then we'll briefly revisit what happens in the brain when we practice it, reviewing the roles of the prefrontal cortex, amygdala, and stress hormones.

Secondly, we'll also return to philosophical meditation, a simple way to clarify our feelings before they cause trouble. Finally, we'll look at how these techniques can fit into our daily life, no incense required, no monastery, no mountain retreat, just a few minutes, a quiet space and you listening up!

12.1 Mindfulness: Where Did It Begin?
12.1.1 Defining Mindfulness

Mindfulness is broadly defined as being present and fully engaged with the current moment; while adopting a non-judgmental and open attitude toward one's experiences.

Rooted in Buddhist meditation practices, mindfulness has evolved into a secular, evidence-based therapeutic approach.
Jon Kabat-Zinn (1994) popularised mindfulness in the West through programmes like Mindfulness-Based Stress Reduction (MBSR), which emphasise the cultivation of awareness and acceptance in everyday activities.

At its core, mindfulness involves two key components:

- **Attention Regulation:** The capacity to focus attention deliberately on the present moment.
- **Attitudinal Orientation:** An openness and acceptance toward one's experiences, including thoughts, emotions and sensations, without undue judgment or reaction.

This dual emphasis creates a mental state where we can observe our internal experiences as transient phenomena rather than permanent attributes of the self. In doing so, mindfulness fosters a balanced perspective that is critical when regulating emotions.

12.1.2 Down to the Root

Historically, mindfulness has its origins in ancient Eastern traditions, particularly within Buddhism. Practices such as Vipassana meditation, which emphasise insight and self-observation, have been integral to achieving greater emotional composure and self-awareness.

Over the decades, Western psychology has embraced many of these concepts; for example, the development of Acceptance and Commitment Therapy (ACT) integrates mindfulness and values-based action to enhance psychological flexibility (Hayes, 2004).

Philosophically, mindfulness challenges the modern tendency toward automatic, habitual reaction. It encourages a deliberate and reflective mode of living, a perspective in which emotions are not suppressed or avoided but rather experienced fully and then observed with curiosity. This stance is thought to diminish the impact of detrimental emotions and reduce the impulsivity that often accompanies emotional dysregulation.

12.1.3 Mindfulness in Contemporary Psychology

Modern research has robustly supported the benefits of mindfulness. Studies have demonstrated that mindfulness-based interventions (MBIs) are effective in reducing stress, anxiety, depression and even chronic pain. Meta-analyses, for example, have shown that MBSR can lead to moderate reductions in anxiety and symptoms of depression across clinical and non-clinical populations (Khoury et al., 2013). In addition, mindfulness has been linked to improved cognitive functioning, such as enhanced working memory, increased attentional capacity and better emotional regulation, suggesting that its benefits extend beyond mere relaxation.

12.2 A Pressure-Release for the Mind

Before frustration explodes into anger or destructive behaviour, it usually starts much more quietly. A knot in the stomach. A vague worry. A feeling you push aside because you're too busy, too tired, or pretending you're fine.

Sadly, emotions do not evaporate, like steam from a boiling pot, just because we ignore them. They build and eventually blow.

The trick is to release that pressure before it erupts. One simple way to do that is through what is known as philosophical meditation. Not the incense-and-cushions kind, though that is fine too, if and when you have the time.

This version is much simpler: you just need to sit down, in a quiet space, for a few minutes and ask yourself, "what is going on in my head?"

You need to take the time to understand yourself, not just the impact of your past but also what's happening in the here and now.

Most meditation advice tells you to quiet the mind. Focus on your breath. Calm the restless "monkey mind." Let thoughts drift away. That's helpful, but philosophical meditation takes a different approach.

Instead of waving goodbye to your thoughts, it invites you to interview them. Because here's the problem: most of what we feel never gets properly processed. It lingers in the background like mental static. Philosophical meditation simply gives that noise a bit of structure by asking these three questions,

1. What am I anxious about right now?

We all worry about something even if we pretend that we don't. Meetings, responsibilities, awkward conversations. The terrifying social nightmares that we brush off and say, "don't really count."

Despite our denial, the anxiety does not disappear. It lingers. Unresolved. When we call them out, clearly recognising them one by one, they start to lose some of their mystery.

Vague dread turns into something concrete. A tangled mess becomes a list to manage. This brings us some peace as lists are strangely comforting to us humans.

2. What am I upset about right now?

We like to think we're tough. Our feathers are never ruffled. Gliding through life unbothered by the seemingly little things. "I am totally fine," we continually mumble to ourselves, hoping that if we repeat it often enough it will remain true.

Meanwhile, we quietly carry disappointment, envy, grief, or hurt. Life delivers small, but steady and continuous, emotional knocks, a message that never arrives, a cold reply, a moment of rejection. We shrug it all off. Afterall we are grown up now, only a baby would get upset about something like that.

The problem is that eventually those shrugged-off feelings pile up and, for what appears to be some unknown reason, we start to feel a bit down, what we might call a "low mood", but it is in fact our static unprocessed emotions that have nowhere to go.

Philosophical meditation helps us to drop the brave face for a moment and admit, at least to ourselves, what's actually bothering us. We don't need to rush. No-one is judging. We just need to start being honest with ourselves.

3. What am I excited or ambitious about right now?

Thankfully not all our static, pent-up emotions relate to hurt feelings or stress. Fortunately, part of the brain, the part that is forever optimistic, is always looking forward into a brighter future.

It might be a book that sparks our curiosity. A super new idea that keeps knocking at the door. A place we suddenly want to visit or someone that inspires us.

Those sparks are not random. They're signals.

Excitement is often our brain quietly saying: this is something good, this matters!

Philosophical meditation is not going to magically fix your life, but it can give the mind space to reorganise itself. At that point, fears become clearer, hurt feels lighter and hope starts to grow.

If you regularly take a few minutes to check in with your mind like this, emotional pressure has a chance to release before it reaches boiling point.

Our destructive reactions don't just appear out of nowhere. They are the result of something that has been building quietly for a long time.

12.3 Emotional Regulation
12.3.1 A Recap: Parts of the Brain that Clock-in

Brain scanning has shown us how the brain responds to mindfulness training.

Key regions of the brain that light up include:

- **Prefrontal Cortex (PFC):** Responsible for executive function, decision-making, and regulating emotional responses. Increased activity in the PFC is associated with enhanced self-regulation and cognitive control.
- **Amygdala:** Involved in the processing of emotional stimuli, particularly fear and anger. Mindfulness practices tend to reduce amygdala reactivity, leading to a dampened emotional response to stress.
- **Anterior Cingulate Cortex (ACC):** Plays a role in conflict monitoring and error detection. Enhanced connectivity between the ACC and the PFC after mindfulness training correlates with improved emotional regulation.

Hölzel et al. (2011) demonstrated that individuals who underwent an eight-week mindfulness meditation programme experienced increased grey matter concentration in the hippocampus, cingulate cortex, and PFC, regions that are essential for learning, memory and regulating emotions.

12.3.2 Recap: Brain Chemistry

Mindfulness practices also impact neurochemical systems. Regular mindfulness meditation has been associated with changes in the levels of key neurotransmitters:

- **Serotonin:** Higher levels are associated with improved mood and reduced aggression.
- **Dopamine:** Regulates the reward system; mindful activities can recalibrate this system, making individuals less reactive to external stressors.
- **Cortisol:** The primary stress hormone, which tends to decrease with regular mindfulness practice, thereby reducing the body's stress response (Hölzel et al., 2011).

These neurochemical changes support a state of balance, allowing us to face challenging emotions with greater calm and self-control.

12.3.3 How Does Neuroplasticity Help Us?

One of the most exciting things about mindfulness is how it reshapes the brain over time. Long-term mindfulness practice actually changes the structure of the brain, strengthening areas linked to emotional regulation, such as increased cortical thickness and improving how brain regions connect. In other words, it's not just a quick stress fix, but something that builds lasting resilience over time.

Regular mindfulness practice has also been shown to lower age-related decline in brain regions linked to focus and self-control.

12.4 Taming the Emotional Storm
12.4.1 Mindfulness Meditation

Mindfulness meditation is one of the most well-known techniques for cultivating presence and reducing emotional reactions.

The practice typically involves sitting quietly, focusing on the breath, and gently redirecting attention back to the present moment whenever distractions arise.

This repeated process of noticing and returning attention is thought to strengthen attention regulation and emotional control.

12.4.2 Get Anchored

Breath awareness meditation focuses on observing the natural rhythm of the breath. This anchors attention to a simple, ever-present bodily process, practitioners learn to stabilise their attention and mitigate the pull of intrusive thoughts or emotional responses.

Even short sessions of breath awareness have been proved to reduce perceived stress and lower cortisol levels.

12.4.3 Body Scan Meditation

The body scan is another mindfulness technique in which attention is systematically directed toward different parts of the body, noticing sensations without judgment.

This practice helps individuals become more aware of physical tension and stress, facilitating a deeper connection between mind and body. The process of routinely scanning the body has been linked to improvements in sleep quality and reductions in anxiety.

12.5 Mindful Movement Practices

Beyond seated meditation, mindful movement integrates awareness into physical activity. Yoga, Tai Chi, and Qi Gong are practices that combine gentle movements with mindful attention and breath control.

These movement-based practices are particularly beneficial for individuals who find sitting meditation challenging or who experience significant body tension as part of their stress response.

For instance, research has shown that yoga can lead to significant improvements in mood and reductions in perceived stress among individuals with anxiety and depression (Field, 2011).

12.5.1 Love Yourself Meditation

Self-compassion, a concept popularised by Neff (2003), is closely linked with mindfulness and has emerged as a critical factor in emotional regulation. Loving-kindness meditation (LKM) involves generating feelings of warmth and goodwill toward oneself and others.

This practice helps counteract harsh self-criticism and cultivates an attitude of acceptance and kindness, which can be particularly valuable during times of failure or disappointment. Studies suggest that LKM increases positive affect, enhances empathy and reduces stress-related biomarkers, making it a powerful tool for taming the emotional storm.

12.5.2 Combining Mindfulness with CBT

Cognitive Behavioural Therapy (CBT) and mindfulness are complementary approaches. While CBT focuses on identifying and restructuring destructive thought patterns, mindfulness encourages a non-judgmental awareness of those thoughts and feelings.

Combining approaches such as Mindfulness-Based Cognitive Therapy (MBCT) integrates elements of both these techniques to help individuals observe counterproductive and detrimental thoughts without becoming entangled in them.

MBCT has been shown to reduce relapse rates in depression and improve overall emotional regulation (Segal, Williams, & Teasdale, 2013).

12.6 Proof That It Works
12.6.1 Clinical Trials

A robust body of research supports the efficacy of mindfulness-based treatments (MBIs) in reducing stress and improving emotional regulation. Meta-analyses have consistently found that MBIs lead to moderate reductions in anxiety and depressive symptoms across diverse populations.

Khoury et al. (2013), for instance, concluded that MBSR and Mindfulness-Based Cognitive Therapy are effective in alleviating symptoms of anxiety and depression.

12.6.2 Snapshot

One patient with chronic generalised anxiety disorder joined an eight-week Mindfulness-Based Stress Reduction (MBSR) programme. By the end, their anxiety had eased noticeably. Their mood was steadier, and they were finally sleeping better.

Brain scans showed that activity in the amygdala, the brain's alarm system, had quietened down, while communication between the prefrontal cortex and the anterior cingulate cortex had strengthened. In other words, the brain's emotional brakes were working more effectively.

Mindfulness has shown similar benefits for people living with chronic pain. By focusing on the present moment and observing pain without immediately fighting it, many patients find that the distress surrounding the pain softens. The pain is still there, but the suffering becomes manageable.

12.6.3 Benefits and Neuroplasticity

Participants in mindfulness training programmes have been found to exhibit increases in cortical thickness in regions associated with attention and sensory processing, as well as improvements in executive function and memory. These neuroplastic changes are associated with enhanced emotional resilience, suggesting that mindfulness not only tames the emotional storm in the moment but also builds long-term capacity to manage stress (Lazar et al., 2005).

12.7 Integrating Mindfulness into Daily Life
12.7.1 Practical Guidelines for Beginners

For individuals new to mindfulness, the initial foray into meditation and mindful practices may seem challenging. That said, here are some simple guidelines that can make the process more accessible:

- **Start Small:** Begin with short, five-to-ten-minute sessions of mindful breathing or a body scan meditation.
- **Create a Routine:** Routine is key. Set aside a specific time each day for mindfulness practice to build a consistent habit.
- **Choose a Quiet Space:** A calm environment free from distractions can enhance focus and facilitate deeper practice.
- **Patience:** Mindfulness is a skill that develops over time. Allow yourself time to experience distractions without frustration, gently guiding your focus back to the present and you.
- **Guided Meditation:** For beginners, guided meditation apps or online videos can provide valuable structure and support.

12.7.2 Advanced Techniques and Mindful Living

As practitioners become more comfortable with basic mindfulness exercises, they can explore advanced techniques and integrate mindfulness into daily activities. For example:

Mindful Walking: Focusing on the sensations of each step, the movement of the body, and the surrounding environment while walking slowly.

- **Mindful Eating:** Paying full attention to the taste, texture, and aroma of food, savouring each bite.
- **Mindfulness in Conversation:** Practicing active listening and being fully present during interactions to enhance communication and empathy.
- **Self-Reflection and Journaling:** Reflecting on experiences throughout the day, noting moments of emotional turbulence and how mindfulness helped or could help mitigate them.

Advanced practitioners may also combine mindfulness with creative activities such as art, music or dance, further enriching their self-expression and emotional awareness.

12.7.3 Getting Digital

As mentioned earlier, apps like Headspace, Calm, and Insight Timer offer simple ways to practise mindfulness, from guided meditations to breathing exercises. They also help build consistency by tracking progress, making it easier to see how regular practice improves emotional control.

12.8 Challenges and Limitations
12.8.1 Response Differences

Despite the numerous benefits, not all individuals respond to mindfulness treatments in the same way. Factors such as personality traits, previous experience with meditative practices and the presence of severe mental health conditions may impact the effectiveness of mindfulness. People, for instance, with high levels of trauma or disconnection might initially find mindfulness practices destabilising and require more thoughtful guidance and support.

12.8.2 Barriers

Practical barriers, such as time constraints and lack of access to trained instructors, may hinder the adoption of mindfulness practices.

Moreover, some people may be sceptical of mindfulness due to its historical roots in religious practices or misconceptions about its purpose.

Addressing these barriers through education, culturally sensitive programming and integration with established therapeutic approaches can help broaden the acceptance of mindfulness across diverse communities.

Conclusion

Mindfulness isn't a trend; it's a skill for navigating real life. It offers practical ways to steady intense emotions, reduce stress and build resilience when things feel overwhelming. Simple practices like meditation, mindful movement and self-compassion don't just help in the moment; they change how we respond to pressure over time.

Whether it is in the classroom or the office, mindfulness is already helping people find a sense of equilibrium in a fast, demanding world. It will not remove life's challenges, but it gives us tools to face them. At its core, mindfulness stops us from reacting on autopilot and empowers us to respond with clarity and choice.

Taming the emotional storm isn't just possible, it's a skill anyone can learn and use every day.

13-
Resilience in the Face of Failure

Introduction

Failure is a part of life. It shows up at school, at work and in relationships. Setbacks are unavoidable, but how we respond to them is not. Some of us recover, others adapt and then there are those that come back even stronger. That is called resilience. Resilience isn't about pushing through at all costs; it's about learning, adjusting and growing when things don't go as planned.

In the following pages we want to explore, with you, what resilience really is and how it's built. We will discuss the thinking patterns, emotional skills and biological processes that help people cope with failure. In a world that moves fast and demands more than ever, resilience matters. It protects mental well-being, supports long-term success and helps to keep us moving forward when things fall apart. The pages that follow break down the key ideas, strategies and evidence behind resilience, so it becomes not just a concept, but a skill that can be learned and used by all of us.

13.1 The Theory of Resilience
13.1.1 Defining Resilience

Resilience is the ability to recover from setbacks, adapt under pressure and sometimes even grow through adversity. It isn't a fixed trait, but a dynamic process shaped by emotional regulation, problem-solving skills, social support and mindset. Masten (2001) describes resilience as "ordinary magic," highlighting that it emerges from everyday protective factors rather than rare personal qualities.

In this view, resilience is not exceptional, it is something most of us can develop through supportive relationships, effective coping strategies and environments that encourage growth.

13.1.2 Theoretical Models Explaining Resilience

Multiple theoretical frameworks contribute to our understanding of resilience:

- **Ecological Systems Theory:** This model emphasises that resilience emerges from the interactions between individuals and their settings, family, school, work and community. Protective factors at each level can buffer against the impacts of failure.
- **Transactional Stress and Coping Model:** Lazarus and Folkman's model (Lazarus, 1991) focus is on cognitive appraisals and coping strategies that determine individuals' responses to stress. According to this model, resilience is bolstered by adaptive appraisal processes, for instance, reframing failure as a challenge rather than a threat.
- **Self-Determination Theory (SDT):** SDT suggests that intrinsic motivation, autonomy, competence and relatedness are essential for psychological well-being. When these needs are met, individuals are more capable of bouncing back from failure.
- **Growth Mindset:** Carol Dweck's work (2006) has shown that when individuals view abilities as malleable rather than fixed, they are more likely to persist in the face of setbacks. This mindset is a crucial predictor of resilience.

Each of the above models provides valuable insights into how resilience is formed and maintained.

13.2 The Mechanisms That Underly Resilience
13.2.1 Cognitive Appraisal and Reframing

We are now fully aware that a key part of resilience is how setbacks are interpreted. Cognitive appraisal, discussed previously, is the way people make sense of stress and failure. When we view setbacks as temporary, specific and changeable, we are more likely to stay motivated and adapt. This process, known as cognitive reframing, helps reduce emotional distress and supports long-term resilience.

Let's look at the example of a student who fails to get a place on a work experience job scheme for talented teens. If he sees this as a challenge rather than a lack of ability, he will be more likely to persist, reapply or apply to another similar scheme and if all fails, try to improve (Lazarus, 1991).

13.2.2 Emotional Regulation and Self-Compassion

Effective regulation of our emotions is essential for coping. Self-compassion, as conceptualised by Neff (2003), involves treating oneself with kindness during times of failure and recognising that imperfection is part of being human.

Individuals with high levels of self-compassion are less likely to spiral into self-criticism after failure. Instead, they can process negative emotions in a constructive manner that promotes recovery and growth.

Mindfulness is particularly effective in enhancing how we control our emotions as it trains us to focus on the present moment without judgment, it also helps us to reduce the intensity of harmful emotional outbursts and overall helps to foster a more resilient mindset.

13.2.3 Attributional Style and Self-Efficacy

The way we attribute causes to our failures significantly influences resilience. A counterproductive attributional style, where failures are seen as personal, permanent and pervasive.

This constant pressure can undermine our confidence in our ability to cope. and lead to a sense of hopelessness. In contrast, if we believe that failures are the result of external or changeable factors, then we tend to maintain higher levels of self-confidence and are more willing to try again. Kim and Park (2020) demonstrated that individuals with healthier ways of explaining failure are more likely to persist after a setback. When combined with a growth mindset, this adaptive attribution fosters a sense of empowerment that is key to resilience.

13.2.4 The Resilient Brain

As we explored in Chapter 1, the brain's emotional alarm system and its regulatory centre work together to shape how we respond to pressure. As we are aware, mindfulness practice can gradually strengthen this balance and those who regularly practise mindfulness tend to become better at noticing stress without immediately reacting to it.

This is an encouraging insight as it reveals that resilience is not simply something you are born with. It is a skill that can be developed. With regular practice and the right support, the brain can learn to respond to difficult situations with greater calm and stability.

The key takeaway is encouraging, resilience is not genetic, it is not a fixed trait. With practice and support, the brain can learn to be more resilient.

13.3 Smarter Ways to Cope
13.3.1 Cognitive-Behavioural Techniques

As we've seen, it's not the setback, it's the story you tell yourself about it. CBT helps you swap "I'm useless" for something more accurate, like "that didn't go well, what can I work on?"

Do that consistently, and you break the self-criticism loop, build confidence, and bounce back faster. Look for what you can fix and break the loop!

13.3.2 Mindfulness-Based Stress Reduction (MBSR)

Mindfulness-Based Stress Reduction (MBSR) is one of the most widely studied mindfulness programmes. It was developed by Jon Kabat-Zinn (1994), and combines guided meditation, gentle yoga, and group discussion to help people develop greater awareness of the present moment. It has been shown that MBSR can significantly reduce stress and anxiety while strengthening psychological resilience (Khoury et al., 2013).

The benefits are especially clear in people living with chronic pain. After completing an eight-week MBSR programme, many patients reported not only less pain, but also better emotional control and greater satisfaction with life.

13.3.3 Self-Compassion Meditation

Self-compassion meditation may sound like a modern wellness invention, but its roots go back centuries to Buddhist compassion practices, especially loving-kindness meditation.

The idea is simple: treat yourself with the same kindness you would show to a good friend. In recent years psychologists such as Kristin Neff and Christopher Germer have translated these ancient ideas into practices like the *Mindful Self-Compassion* programme, bringing a little more kindness and a little less self-criticism into modern psychology.

At its heart, self-compassion meditation asks us to make three small but powerful shifts. First, notice what you're feeling rather than pretending everything is fine, second, speak to yourself with kindness instead of running the usual inner critic commentary and third, remember a comforting truth: being imperfect is not a personal failure, it is the human condition.

Everyone falls or stumbles at some point in life, and occasionally we can make a spectacular mess. That said, this simple shift can make a real difference. People who practice self-compassion tend to experience less anxiety, depression, and stress, and they bounce back from difficulties more easily.

Brain studies even suggest that when we respond to ourselves with kindness, the brain's threat system settles down while circuits linked to emotional regulation and care become more active. In other words, self-compassion doesn't make us soft, it actually helps us become calmer, steadier, and better equipped to handle life when we accidentally end up at a dead end.

3.3.4 Social Support

Spending time with the right people helps. A lot. The right support can calm you down, challenge distorted thinking, and remind you you're not alone. Strong supportive networks help you to cope better and lower stress.

13.3.5 Recap: Growing A Growth Mindset

A growth mindset is the difference between "I failed" and "I'm learning." See ability as something you build, not something you either have or don't have, that way setbacks stop being the end of your story. If, as a society, we promote educational programmes, workshops, and coaching that reinforce this mindset, we can help people recover more quickly and grow stronger when they hit a bump in the road

Conclusion

Resilience isn't just about surviving failure; it's about using life's adversities as fuel for growth. We have now explored ways to build resilience through practices like cognitive reframing, mindfulness, self-compassion, philosophical reflection, supportive relationships, and a growth mindset.

We have discovered that resilience is not a fixed trait. It's a process shaped by both inner skills and the support around us. When we stop seeing failure as a verdict on our worth and start seeing it as useful feedback, recovery becomes easier and growth often follows.

Of course, there's no single formula. These strategies can be adapted to different lives and challenges, whether you're a student, professional, parent, or athlete, with practice, and with people who support us, resilience can grow even after repeated difficulties. In a world that often feels like a pressure cooker, learning healthier ways to cope is essential, not just for us, our families and friends, but to also build stronger communities. Resilience is both personal and shared. With the right support, life's storms don't just pass; they leave us wiser and stronger.

-14-

When Conflict Presents Opportunity

Introduction

Conflict is inherent in all human interactions and takes many forms. Aggression, for instance, when it is misdirected or unresolved leads to destructive outcomes. Nonetheless, within the realm of conflict resolution lies a transformative potential: the ability to convert destructive aggression into constructive dialogue. This transformation is not merely about quelling conflict, but about reorienting adversarial interactions into opportunities for empowerment, mutual understanding and lasting change.

As discussed earlier, frustration, social comparison, and perceived threat can intensify conflict and trigger aggressive responses. Building on these ideas, this chapter will examine how such impulses can be redirected through structured conflict-resolution approaches.

Drawing on theories already introduced, including the frustration–aggression hypothesis, social comparison theory, and transformative mediation, we will explore the cognitive, emotional, and biological processes that shape conflict and consider how they can be used to guide more constructive outcomes.

We will also include some examples where transformative conflict resolution approaches have been successful and review specific techniques such as active listening, empathy training, assertive communication and structured dialogue, which have been shown to de-escalate tensions and facilitate mutual recognition.

The goal of this chapter is twofold: to provide a robust conceptual framework for understanding how transformative conflict resolution works and to offer actionable strategies for turning aggression into constructive dialogue.

14.1 Understanding Conflict and Transformation
14.1.1 Classical Theories of Aggression and Conflict

Where does aggression come from? Animals can be aggressive, but humans add a few extra ingredients, ego, identity, culture, and occasionally wounded pride. We're also the only species that hold a grudge, and maybe even dream up a little revenge.

One early explanation, the frustration–aggression hypothesis, suggests people become frustrated when their goals are blocked. If they are unable to confront the real source of their frustration, perhaps because of social rules, hierarchy, or fear of consequences, they may redirect their anger toward someone safer or less threatening.

However, later research showed the story is not quite so simple. Aggression is not always inevitable; it's shaped by how we interpret the situation and the environment we find ourselves in.

Social comparison theory adds another layer. When we constantly compare ourselves with people who seem more successful, the gap between who we are and who we think we should be can start to sting.

If those feelings of inadequacy are not managed, they can chip away at our self-perception and occasionally spill over into resentment or hostility.

14.1.2 A Paradigm Shift

Transformative mediation, as developed by Bush and Folger (2005), represents a significant departure from traditional conflict resolution models that aim solely at problem-solving or settlement. Instead, transformative approaches focus on empowerment and recognition.

This model suggests that conflicts can serve as opportunities for transformation by facilitating a deeper understanding of each party's needs and values.

Rather than viewing aggression as a hindrance, transformative mediation sees it as an expression of unmet needs that, if properly understood and addressed, can lead to mutual growth.

Key components of transformative mediation include:

- **Empowerment:** Enabling individuals to speak for themselves and reclaim their voice during conflict.
- **Recognition:** Fostering mutual understanding by encouraging parties to acknowledge each other's perspectives and emotional experiences.
- **Constructive Dialogue:** Creating a space where parties move beyond blame to identify shared interests and collaborative solutions.

This model aligns with broader humanistic and relational frameworks, suggesting that when participants in a conflict are given opportunities to reevaluate their positions and express vulnerability, aggressive impulses can be transformed into constructive dialogue.

14.1.3 A Recap: Twisting the Narrative

As discussed earlier, cognitive dissonance kicks in when our actions clash with how we see ourselves, so we justify, reframe, or shift the blame. That blame game only deepens the conflict and shuts down real dialogue. Transformative conflict resolution cuts through this by slowing things down, challenging bias, and creating space for a more constructive conversation.

14.2 The Hidden Forces Behind Conflict
14.2.1 The Neurobiology of Aggression

As we explored earlier, conflict isn't just psychological, it's biological. Under pressure, the brain's emotional alarm system can take over, driving quick, reactive responses, especially when reality doesn't match expectations.

14.2.2 Empathy, and Constructive Dialogue

Managing our emotions is a key factor in turning aggression into constructive dialogue. When we can manage our responses, through strategies such as mindful breathing, reframing damaging thoughts or engaging in self-compassion, we are more likely to enter talks with compassion and empathy.

Empathy allows each party to view the conflict from the perspective of the other, thereby reducing defensive postures and opening the way for genuine recognition and mutual understanding.
It has been consistently shown that increased empathy correlates with higher rates of conflict resolution and improved outcomes.

14.2.3 Losing Our Cool

Chronic stress, marked by constantly high cortisol, can wear down thinking and fuel impulsive aggression. When the stress response stays switched on, self-control slips, making it harder to pause or talk things through. Stress-reducing practices that activate the parasympathetic nervous system, like mindfulness, help dial this back, cutting aggressive outbursts and supporting calmer, more deliberate responses during a conflict.

14.3 A Better Way to Handle Conflict
14.3.1 Active Listening and Reflection

At the heart of transformative conflict resolution is active listening, really hearing the other person and reflecting it back.

This shifts the focus from winning the argument to understanding, with the main emphasis being on understanding, and it helps to cool things down fast!

It can be as simple as restating key points, asking for clarification or calling out the emotions you hear and feel.

When trying to communicate in a conflictual situation, active listening can build empathy and reduce hostility.

Scenario: At work a dispute over project responsibilities arises, a manager who employs active listening might say,
"I hear you're feeling overwhelmed with the current workload. Can you tell me more about what's causing this pressure?"

Now the focus is on understanding, and the manager can facilitate a calm discussion that leads to identifying practical solutions.

14.3.2 Empathy Training and Shifting Perspective

Empathy training involves exercises designed to improve one's ability to understand and share the feelings of others. Techniques such as role-playing or narrative exchanges help parties see conflict from a new perspective, seeing matters from the other party's point of view. Studies indicate that structured empathy training can lead to significant reductions in aggression and improve conflict resolution. (Bush & Folger, 2005).

Scenario: A community mediation programme might invite disputing parties to engage in a "perspective switch" exercise, this is where each participant articulates what they believe the other is feeling.

This method fosters mutual recognition and can lower emotional barriers to discussion.

14.3.3 Cognitive Reappraisal and Conflict Reframing

Cognitive reappraisal is a technique central to many cognitive-behavioural approaches. It involves changing one's interpretation of a conflict from one of threat and blame to one of opportunity for learning and growth.

When the conflict is reframed, individuals can reduce the intensity of their emotional responses and open up to constructive dialogue. This process is critical in mitigating the effects of cognitive dissonance that arise from conflicting self-images during disputes.

Scenario: In a marital conflict over household responsibilities, rather than interpreting a partner's complaint as an attack on one's character, one might reframe it as an expression of a desire for more balance. This reframing can transform a potentially destructive conflict into a conversation about equitable division of labour.

14.3.4 Negotiation & Collaborative Problem-Solving

One effective way to resolve conflict is to combine negotiation with a collaborative approach.

Instead of trying to "win" the argument, the parties work together to find solutions that benefit everyone involved.

This means identifying shared interests, exploring possible solutions, and pooling resources to address the underlying problem.

Negotiation theory states that these combined approaches, where both sides look for mutual gains, are far more effective at maintaining positive relationships and preventing future conflict than simple win–lose strategies.

Scenario: Imagine a team arguing over how to allocate limited resources. Rather than competing for the largest share, a facilitated meeting allows everyone to explain their key needs.

The group can then work together to develop a plan that supports both individual priorities and the team's overall goals.

14.4 Snapshots: Transforming Aggression into Constructive Dialogue
14.4.1 The Turnaround of a High-Pressure Team

Background

In a large technology firm, a division characterised by intense competition and high-performance expectations was experiencing severe internal conflict. Team members frequently engaged in aggressive exchanges and the aggressive behaviour of a few key individuals had led to falling morale and decreased productivity.

Approach

A comprehensive conflict resolution programme was introduced, which incorporated elements of active listening, empathy training and negotiation.

The programme included:
- Regular discussions where employees practiced active listening.
- Role-playing exercises to help team members understand the emotional states and perspectives of their colleagues.
- Structured problem-solving sessions focused on identifying shared goals rather than individual wins.

Outcome

Over a six-month period, the team reported significant improvements in communication and a reduction in aggressive incidents. Productivity metrics improved markedly, and employee satisfaction surveys indicated a renewed sense of cohesion and shared purpose.

This scenario demonstrates that even in a high-pressure competitive environment, transformative conflict resolution can recalibrate interpersonal dynamics and foster a collaborative spirit.

14.4.2 Repairing Relationships Through Dialogue

Background

A family experiencing recurring conflict, exacerbated by misdirected anger stemming from work-related stress, sought to resolve deep-seated issues that were affecting marital satisfaction and parent–child relationships. The aggressive outbursts and chronic misunderstandings had led to emotional distancing and increased household tension.

Approach

A trained mediator introduced transformative conflict resolution techniques, including:

- Guided family meetings to create a safe environment for discussion.
- Active listening exercises where each family member was encouraged to express their feelings and then repeat back what they heard.
- Empathy-building activities that focused on recognising the stressors external to the family, reducing the tendency to blame one another.

Outcome

Within a few months, the family reported a notable reduction in arguments. The mediator's use of reflective dialogue and perspective-taking exercises allowed family members to understand the external pressures influencing behaviour and to de-escalate aggressive responses.

Long-term follow-up indicated improved emotional closeness and a more supportive home environment, illustrating the transformative power of conflict resolution within the family.

14.4.3 Mediating Social Tensions

Background

In an urban neighbourhood characterised by economic disparities and high social tension, recurring conflicts between community groups had led to sporadic outbreaks of violence and social fragmentation.

The absence of effective communication channels and prevailing stereotypes fuelled misdirected aggression, often resulting in unintended harm to marginalised residents.

Approach

A community mediation programme was launched that brought together leaders from different parts of the community.

The approach included:

- Training sessions in transformative mediation techniques.
- Community discussion structured around shared concerns rather than divisive narratives.
- Collaborative projects designed to build intergroup solidarity and achieve common community goals.

Outcome

The programme succeeded in reducing overt aggression and fostering a culture of constructive dialogue.

Community members developed skills in active listening, empathy and collaborative problem-solving. Eventually, the neighbourhood experienced improved trust between groups, a decline in violent incidents, and increased participation in community-building projects. It shows how conflict resolution can heal both individual disputes and wider community challenges.

14.5 Guidelines for Conflict Resolution

14.5.1 Establishing a Supportive Framework

The following steps are critical when creating a safe and neutral environment for transformative conflict resolution.

- **Neutral Facilitation:** Employ trained mediators who can maintain neutrality and guide discussions without bias.
- **Confidentiality:** Ensure that all parties feel secure in sharing their perspectives without fear of reprisal.
- **Structured Dialogue:** Use predetermined formats, for example, each member has their turn to speak, to ensure that everyone has a chance to speak and be heard.
- **Clear Objectives:** Define the goals of the mediation process, whether it is to restore relationships, clarify misunderstandings or develop joint action plans.

14.5.2 Techniques for Active Listening and Empathy

- **Reflective Listening:** Encourage each party to paraphrase what they heard, ensuring accurate understanding of feelings and needs.
- **Emotion Identification:** Teach participants to name their emotions and those of others, fostering clarity and reducing miscommunication.
- **Perspective-Taking Exercises:** Use role reversal or "walk in my shoes" exercises to help each party appreciate the impact of their words and actions on others.
- **Non-Verbal Communication:** Emphasise the importance of body language, eye contact, and other non-verbal cues that promote empathy and connection.

14.5.3 Developing a Conflict Resolution Protocol

A well-designed conflict resolution protocol provides a blueprint for addressing disputes:

- **Early Intervention:** Implement systems for early detection of conflict, for example, regular feedback sessions and conflict hotlines.
- **Stepwise Escalation:** Outline clear steps for resolving minor disagreements before they escalate into major conflicts.
- **Mediation Processes:** Include guidelines for when and how to involve professional mediators or facilitators.
- **Follow-Up Mechanisms:** Establish mechanisms for monitoring progress after resolution, ensuring that agreements are sustained and that any recurring issues are addressed promptly.

14.5.4 Training and Capacity Building

Organisations, schools and community groups should invest in training programmes that build capacity in conflict resolution:

- **Workshops and Seminars:** Regular training sessions in transformative mediation, active listening and empathy.
- **Peer Mentoring:** Pair experienced mediators with novices to build skills through practical, on-the-job training.
- **Simulation Exercises:** Use role-playing scenarios to simulate conflict and practice resolution techniques in a controlled environment.
- **Evaluation and Feedback:** Continuously assess the effectiveness of training programmes, incorporating feedback from participants to refine techniques.

14.6 Impact of Transformative Conflict Resolution
14.6.1 Quantitative Metrics

Assessment of conflict resolution techniques can be achieved through various quantitative measures:

- **Surveys and Scales:** Tools such as the Conflict Resolution Styles Inventory and the Interpersonal Reactivity Index can measure changes in attitudes and behaviours before and after.
- **Productivity Metrics:** In organisational settings, reductions in absenteeism, staff turnover and conflict-related downtime are indicators of improved relationships.
- **Psychological Assessments:** Measures of stress, anxiety and overall well-being before and after resolution processes can quantify personal improvements.

14.6.2 Qualitative Evaluations

In addition to quantitative metrics, qualitative methods provide deep insights into participants' experiences:

- **Interviews and Focus Groups:** Engaging participants in reflective discussions about how the resolution process affected their relationships can reveal nuanced changes that numbers alone might miss.
- **Case Narratives:** Detailed documentation of specific conflict resolution cases can help elucidate mechanisms and best practice.
- **Follow-Up:** Tracking relationships over extended periods to assess the lasting impact of resolution approaches applied.

Research by van Veen et al. (2009) shows that to really understand and improve conflict resolution programmes, we need to look at people's real experiences.

14.7 Challenges and Limitations
14.7.1 Resistance to Change

Not everyone is open to working through conflict with conversation.

Longstanding mistrust, cultural differences and power imbalances can get in the way.

Breaking through that resistance often means slowly building trust and showing early wins that change attitudes.

14.7.2 The Bigger Picture

How well conflict resolution works depends a lot on the setting. What works at the office may fail at home. To be effective, approaches must be customised to fit the values and power dynamics of the group, although that kind of tailoring takes time and resources.

14.7.3 Resource Constraints

Putting transformative conflict resolution into practice takes time, skill and often money. In low-resource settings, that can make it hard to roll out consistently. Research and scalable training are key to lowering those barriers.

14.7.4. From Reacting to Connecting

Transformative conflict resolution starts from a simple idea: the energy behind aggression does not have to explode, it can be redirected into a constructive discussion. If we focus on empowerment, mutual recognition and empathy, adversarial moments can turn into real opportunities for growth.

The key takeaways should be:

- **Empowerment and Recognition:** Helping people share matters from their perspective and actually see the person on the other side, this is at the heart of transforming conflict.
- **Active Listening and Empathetic Engagement:** Techniques that promote reflection and mutual understanding are essential for de-escalating aggression.
- **Collaborative Problem-Solving:** Shifting the focus from blame to shared goals allows conflicting parties to work together toward mutually beneficial outcomes.
- **Setting-Sensitive Approaches:** Tailoring approaches to the specific cultural and organisational setting is crucial for success.

By integrating these principles, transformative conflict resolution offers a powerful framework for not only mitigating the fallout from aggression but also for fostering resilient, trusting relationships across diverse settings.

Conclusion

Unresolved conflict, especially when it turns aggressive, can take a real toll on personal well-being, workplace effectiveness and social cohesion. However, that same energy doesn't have to stay destructive.

When channelled through transformative conflict resolution, it can fuel constructive dialogue and meaningful change. We have now explored the theories behind conflict and cognitive processes that drive aggression and revealed some of the practical tools that help shift adversarial interactions towards a healthier direction.

Looking ahead, investing in conflict resolution training, creating supportive environments and using new technologies are more important than ever. Challenges like resistance to change and limited resources remain, but ongoing research and innovation continue.

Ultimately, transformative conflict resolution isn't about getting rid of conflict, it's about learning how to handle it well. When empowerment, mutual recognition and collaboration is prioritised we can turn aggression's destructive potential into a discussion that resolves disputes and deepens our understanding of one another.

Cultivating a Culture of Emotional Intelligence

Introduction

In a world shaped by rapid tech change, globalisation and everyday complexity, the ability to recognise, understand and manage emotions, our own and others', has become essential. Emotional intelligence (EI) is no longer a "soft skill." It is a core capability that supports healthy relationships, learning and performance at work. It is now acknowledged that a higher EI strengthens community resilience and improves how people handle relationships, support one another and resolve disputes. Building a culture of emotional intelligence isn't just about training individuals. It also means shaping policies, organisational structures and social environments that consistently value empathy, self-awareness and flexible emotional regulation.

Now let's look ahead and explore how emotional intelligence (EI) can become part of everyday life.

First, we will delve into what EI really means and where it originates. Then we'll look at the psychology and brain science behind it, including how it helps us adapt and stay resilient.

Next, we'll explore some scenarios to understand how EI can be built into culture through training and preventive strategies that boost well-being.

Finally, we'll map out practical ways to create environments where EI is actively nurtured and conflicts are handled constructively, so people can truly thrive in an increasingly connected world.

Pressure Cooker

15.1. Shaped by our Past
15.1.1 Emotional Beings

We are all emotional beings with a long history and our own unique list of tragedies, betrayals and injustices. We are complicated, proprietors of a tangled narrative, sentinels of the unspoken.

Quietly but steadily, our past shapes who we are, who we become, how we behave and more importantly how we react.

The trouble is, we are mostly unaware of how much this inheritance is steering our judgments, often at great personal cost.

Our past doesn't stay, where it should, in the past. It leaks into the present, bending how we read a friend's silence, decide what we're responsible for, or judge how much permission we need to take up space.

We respond to today through expectations formed long ago, even though we have forgotten where or how those expectations originated.

We are especially vulnerable to this bizarre process, because childhood lasts so long. As children we spend nearly two decades growing up, and many years, if not all our lives, under the close influence of our parents.

Other species get on with it much more quickly, a foal is up on its feet thirty minutes after birth, over ninety-seven per cent of fish lay thousands or millions of eggs, simply to swim off and never see their offspring again, even the blue whale, (*Balaenoptera musculus*), a marine mammal and the largest animal to have ever lived on the planet is independent by five.

We, by contrast, barely manage to speak before two and take almost twenty years before we are actually declared adults.

15.1.2 Time Will Tell

All that time leaves a mark. Home, and more importantly, the people who run it, our parents, shape us deeply. We absorb moods, tones, habits, tensions. We remember the feel of the carpet, the smell of cupboards, the sound a parent makes when concentrating. Years later, we can return to our childhood home as adults and suddenly feel a child again.

Psychology has shown how powerfully this hidden past continues to operate. One famous example is the Rorschach ink blot test, where people describe what they see in ambiguous images.

The images mean nothing in themselves, but our responses reveal much about how we see the world.

What do you see in Hermann Rorschachs inkblot test (1932) below?

Scary Giant or Cute Bunny?

Someone raised with warmth might see a mask with kind eyes and floppy ears giving an atmosphere of kindness and playfulness.

Someone shaped by a hounding, critical, domineering parent might see a heavy built, powerful figure with a head leaning forward as if ready to attack.

Genuine adulthood begins when we recognise how our childhood can still pull our strings and condition our reactions.

Maturity, on the other hand, is trying, however flawed, to see the present clearly, without letting the past do all the talking.

15.2 Defining Emotional Intelligence
15.2.1 Evolution of the EI Concept

Emotional intelligence came into focus in the 1990s, when researchers like Mayer and Salovey (1997) and Daniel Goleman (1995) showed that managing your own emotions, and understanding others', can matter just as much as traditional intelligence.

While IQ tests emphasise logic and analytical thinking, EI focuses on skills like self-awareness, emotional regulation, empathy, motivation and social skills. These abilities play a key role in building relationships and succeeding both personally and professionally.

15.2.2 Key Components of Emotional Intelligence

According to the framework proposed by Mayer and Salovey (1997), emotional intelligence comes down to four key abilities.

First, perceiving emotions, accurately recognising feelings in ourselves and others, whether through facial expressions, body language, or tone of voice.

Second, using emotions, tapping into feelings to support thinking, problem-solving, and decision-making.

Third, understanding emotions, grasping why emotions arise, how they change over time, and where they might lead.

Fourth, managing emotions, regulating our own feelings while responding to others in ways that guide interactions more constructively.

Daniel Goleman (1995) expanded these concepts into five domains, often summarised as self-awareness, self-regulation, motivation, empathy and social skills. Each model contributes valuable insights into how EI can be applied, taught and measured.

15.2.3 EI as a Predictor of Success and Well-Being

Extensive research has linked high levels of EI to improved outcomes in multiple areas. In the workplace, emotionally intelligent leaders are better at managing teams, resolving conflicts and promoting a positive organisational culture (Goleman, 1998). In educational settings, students with higher EI tend to have better academic performance, stronger interpersonal relationships and lower rates of behavioural problems. On a personal level, EI is associated with lower incidences of depression and anxiety and greater overall resilience. As such, cultivating EI is not merely an individual asset, it is a fundamental building block for healthy, productive communities.

15.3 The Psychological and Neurobiological Foundations of EI
15.3.1 The Next Generation of Emotional Regulation

Recent advances in neuroscience are reshaping how we understand and manage emotional reactions. Neuroimaging studies have shown that patterns of activity between key brain regions, particularly those involved in emotional response and regulation, differ in people who struggle with impulsive or aggressive reactions. These findings suggest that emotional regulation is not simply a matter of willpower, but also of how effectively these brain regions communicate.

This has led to growing interest in approaches that actively "train" these areas of the brain. Techniques such as biofeedback and neurofeedback allow individuals to observe and gradually influence their own physiological and neural responses in real time, strengthening their ability to regulate reactions under pressure.

As increased knowledge is gained in this area, a more profound understanding proves that these combined approaches provide individuals with an improved ability to reduce misguided and disproportionate reactions and build long-term resilience.

15.3.2 Cognitive Processes Underpinning EI

People with high emotional intelligence tend to be strong at metacognition, the ability to step back and reflect on their own thoughts and feelings. This awareness helps them reframe challenges in less threatening ways. Instead of seeing a setback at work as a personal failure, for example, they're more likely to view it as a chance to learn and grow.

Cognitive-behavioural research shows that this kind of reframing softens the emotional hit of stress and supports more constructive coping strategies (Lazarus, 1991).

15.3.3 The Brain Behind Emotional Control

Modern research continues to deepen our understanding of how the brain supports emotional intelligence. As discussed earlier, effective emotional regulation relies on the interaction between brain systems responsible for emotional reactivity and those involved in control and reflection.

When these systems are well coordinated, individuals are better able to manage strong emotions and respond more thoughtfully in challenging situations.

As we have learnt, in previous chapters, mindfulness, now widely incorporated into emotional intelligence training, can strengthen this capacity over time. Studies, including Hölzel et al. (2011), indicate that regular practice is associated with measurable changes in brain regions linked to attention and emotional processing. The observed benefits of emotional intelligence development, include effective stress management, greater emotional control, and stronger relationships.

15.3.4 Emotional Resilience

Resilient people tend to be emotionally stable or have the ability to bounce back quickly when the going gets tough. At the core of that resilience is emotional control, which is the ability to notice emotions, make sense of them, and respond appropriately.

Strategies like reappraisal, mindfulness, and self-compassion can strongly improve emotional intelligence and improve mental health. When our mindset is changed and challenges are seen as temporary setbacks rather than total failures, a new positive cycle of growth is created helping us to cope in a healthier way.

15.4 Cultivating a Culture of Emotional Intelligence
15.4.1 Leadership's Role in Cultivating EI

Leaders play a big role in shaping a culture of emotional intelligence. Emotionally intelligent leaders model self-awareness and empathy while creating spaces where open communication and constructive feedback are the norm. Studies show that transformational leadership, focused on vision, inspiration and genuine consideration, is linked to higher employee EI and stronger performance (Goleman, 1998).

Leaders can reinforce this by rolling out EI training, encouraging coaching and mentoring, and putting policies in place that recognise and reward emotionally supportive behaviour. Finally, these practices shift organisational norms and help EI take root across the whole organisation.

15.4.2 Educational Initiatives to Build EI

Emotional intelligence is best developed early. Schools that use social-emotional learning (SEL) programmes see better student behaviour, stronger academic performance and healthier relationships. SEL teaches core skills like recognising emotions, empathy, problem-solving and responsible decision-making. Durlak et al. (2011) found that students in SEL programmes showed improved social behaviour and lower emotional distress.

Bringing EI into the classroom benefits more than just students, it helps create calmer, more resilient school environments. When teachers model EI through active listening, empathy and constructive feedback, they reinforce these skills in everyday interactions, setting up students with the ability to manage and reflect on their feelings for life.

15.4.3 Community-Based Approaches

At a community level, cultivating a culture of EI involves creating spaces where empathy, open dialogue, and supportive relationships can be prioritised. Community resources that provide group-based techniques, such as mindfulness workshops, conflict resolution training and peer support groups can enhance EI. Polarisation within communities can be reduced by improving human connection and addressing social stressors through collaborative initiatives. Government and charitable entities can collaborate to create public policies that promote emotional well-being. Efforts to reduce social isolation, increase participation within the community and provide mental health support are all preventive strategies that contribute to improved EI.

15.5 Building EI
15.5.1 Early Identification

Prevention is central to building a culture of emotional intelligence. Spotting emotional challenges early makes it easier to step in before unhealthy patterns take hold. In schools, regular check-ins on social-emotional skills and mental health help educators intervene sooner. In workplaces, employee assistance programmes (EAPs) that include EI assessments and stress-management workshops can flag risks like burnout and conflict early on.

If we can start making these assessments part of everyday life in schools and organisations, leaders can focus on prevention and strengthening resilience before problems escalate.

15.5.2 Leveraging Technology

Today, with technological developments, like smart watches and other wearable devices, we can access real-time insights into how our bodies respond when under stress. Some medical technologies go even further, for instance, non-invasive Doppler devices such as the USCOM 1A allow trained clinicians to assess cardiovascular function in real time, supporting faster diagnosis and treatment when the body is under strain.

While most people will never need to interact directly with these clinical devices, the advantage gained is important. The faster we detect what's happening inside our body, the earlier we can respond.

This shift from reactive to preventive care is changing how we understand and manage stress, both in healthcare and everyday life.

15.5.3 Continuous Training and Capacity Building

Resilience and emotional intelligence are not static; they are dynamic capabilities that require continuous development. Ongoing training programmes, such as workshops, seminars, and coaching sessions, should be integral components of organisational and educational strategies. Continuous professional development not only reinforces key EI skills but also encourages a growth mindset and allows individuals to understand that their emotional abilities can be improved through sustained effort.

Long-term benefits gained by organisations that invest in training programmes are higher levels of employee well-being, lower staff turnover rates and enhanced innovation.

Similarly, educational institutions that embed SEL across the curriculum contribute to more emotionally resilient students who are better prepared to face the challenges of life.

15.5.4 Fostering Inclusive Cultures

Inclusivity sits at the heart of a culture of emotional intelligence. When we feel accepted, included and free to speak openly, we are more likely to feel valued and supported.

Policies like anti-bullying programmes in schools or diversity and inclusion initiatives at work help signal that emotional well-being matters.

If leaders also show vulnerability and genuine care, they will set the tone for empathy and make constructive conflict resolution the norm.

15.5.5 Collaborative Public Health Initiatives

Integrating EI into public health initiatives offers a powerful preventive strategy. Programmes that combine mental health education with community-building activities have the potential to mitigate the adverse effects of stress, depression and anxiety.

Such initiatives can include public workshops, community mindfulness sessions and campaigns that educate citizens about the importance of managing their feelings.

15.6 Snapshots: How to Cultivate an EI Culture
15.6.1 Educate EI: A School District's Journey

Background

A large urban school district identified that declining student engagement and rising behavioural issues were linked to low emotional intelligence levels. Recognising the long-term implications for academic achievement and social cohesion, district leaders initiated a comprehensive social and emotional learning (SEL) programme across all schools.

Approach

The programme wove social and emotional learning (SEL) into everyday school life. In the classroom, students learned practical skills like regulating emotions, showing empathy, and resolving conflicts.

Teachers received training on how to model emotional intelligence and create classrooms that support emotional growth. Families were brought in through workshops and resources so the same skills could be reinforced at home. Local mental health organisations partnered with schools to provide extra guidance, support, and resources.

Outcome

Over a three-year period, the district observed significant improvements in academic performance, reduced disciplinary incidents and enhanced student well-being. Students indicated that they felt more confident and better able to manage stress, evidence that cultivating a culture of EI has lasting benefits.

15.6.2 Corporate Reinvention: A Tech Company's Emotional Intelligence Initiative

Background

A prominent technology company faced challenges with employee burnout, high turnover and internal conflict. In response, senior management launched an EI initiative aimed at reshaping the corporate culture.

Approach

The company embedded emotional intelligence into everyday work. Employees joined workshops on active listening, mindful communication, and managing stress.

Managers received leadership coaching focused on empathy, empowerment, and transformational leadership. Regular employee feedback helped track stress levels and team dynamics, allowing the training to evolve as needed. A mobile app supported the effort by offering guided mindfulness, mood tracking, and quick access to additional mental health resources.

Outcome

Within one year, the company reported a marked reduction in internal conflicts. Productivity increased, and employee satisfaction surveys reflected improved morale and a greater sense of belonging. This scenario helps to highlight the transformative impact of embedding EI into corporate culture as a preventive strategy against stress and conflict.

15.6.3 Community Empowerment

In a diverse urban neighbourhood facing social fragmentation and economic disparities, community leaders recognised that the lack of emotional intelligence skills among residents was contributing to recurring disputes and a breakdown in communal bonds.

Approach

The initiative brought emotional intelligence into the heart of the community. Free workshops taught practical skills like conflict resolution, empathy, and mindfulness.

Trained peer mediators helped people in conflict talk things through and rebuild trust. Local media and social networks shared stories of resilience and collective problem-solving.

Youth programmes focused on social-emotional learning and constructive communication, helping the next generation build stronger, healthier communities.

Outcome

Over a two-year period, the neighbourhood experienced fewer incidents of violence and vandalism, improved neighbourhood satisfaction and stronger social ties.

The success of these approaches reinforced the idea that nurturing EI at the community level can create a resilient, harmonious environment that benefits everyone.

15.6.4 When Communities Fail to Respond

Background

Late one afternoon, a mother receives the call no parent ever wants. Her ten-year-old daughter, who had been out riding her bike, has been struck by a car and was killed instantly. Shock and grief overwhelm her.

Approach

The surrounding community is disconnected and struggles to respond. Some neighbours feel unsure about what to say. Others worry about intruding. A few send brief messages of sympathy but assume someone else will step in to help.

No one visits the mother. The house remains silent as she tries to process the unimaginable alone.

Without emotional awareness or coordinated support, the days that follow become increasingly isolating. The mother is left to navigate profound grief without the human connection that can help anchor someone in a crisis.

Outcome

In the absence of support, the mother's despair deepens. The isolation compounds the trauma of the loss. Eventually, overwhelmed by grief and loneliness, she takes her own life. When emotional intelligence is absent at the community level, tragedy can escalate. Lack of a coordinated collective response can leave individuals dangerously alone in moments when support matters most.

15.6.5 The Power of a Caring Community

Background

A mother receives devastating news: her ten-year-old daughter, who had been out riding her bike, has been struck by a car and killed instantly.

The shock is immediate and overwhelming. Her younger son is still at school, unaware of what has happened. The situation is every parent's worst nightmare, sudden loss, confusion, and unbearable grief.

Approach

In this neighbourhood, people have developed a culture of emotional awareness and care. When the news spreads, neighbours respond thoughtfully and quickly.

One person goes to sit with the mother, offering quiet presence rather than words. Another contacts the school and arranges to collect her son before he hears the news from someone else.

Others organise practical help, cooking meals, answering calls and other household chores.

No one tries to minimise the tragedy or rush the grieving process. Instead, people listen, allow space for grief and sadness, and offer steady and consistent support. During the following weeks, the community continues to check in gently, making sure the mother and her son remain surrounded by care, compassion, and practical help.

Outcome

The grief is profound and life-changing, but the mother is not left to face it alone. The community's empathy, awareness, and coordinated support create a protective network around the family. This collective emotional intelligence does not remove the pain of the loss, but it helps carry the emotional weight, giving space to heal.

Cultivating an emotionally intelligent environment means creating communities where people notice distress, respond with empathy, and act with care. While such a culture cannot prevent tragedy, it can profoundly shape how individuals are supported through it, and whether or not they face their darkest moments alone.

15.7 Towards A More Emotionally Intelligent World
15.7.1 Building a Smarter Emotional Culture

The evidence throughout this chapter points to a clear takeaway: prioritising emotional intelligence pays off. EI-rich environments support better well-being, greater creativity and stronger resilience. Building a more emotionally intelligent society ultimately means committing to ongoing learning and weaving prevention into everyday practice at every level.

15.7.2 Turning Challenges into Opportunities

One of the most powerful lessons emerging from resilience and EI research is that setbacks and failures can be transformed into opportunities for growth and improvement. When we embrace a growth mindset, fostering supportive relationships and maintaining a commitment to self-awareness and empathy, we and by extension, our communities, can convert adversity into a catalyst for positive change.

15.7.3 A Roadmap for Change

The roadmap to cultivating a culture of emotional intelligence involves:
- Implementing changes in all public and private entities.
- Investing in ongoing professional development and mental health resources.
- Leveraging technology to scale and personalise EI education.
- Engaging stakeholders at all levels, from policymakers to grassroots, to champion the value of emotional intelligence.

Conclusion

Building a culture of emotional intelligence offers a powerful path toward more resilient, empathetic and connected societies. As this chapter has shown, emotional intelligence (EI) isn't just an individual skill, it's a shared resource that can reduce conflict, strengthen relationships and support lasting personal and professional growth.

The evidence is clear: EI improves learning, lowers workplace stress and boosts community well-being, making the case for embedding it into everyday life stronger than ever.

Looking ahead, the focus is on expanding what already works while exploring new, innovative approaches, especially those that draw on technology and cross-disciplinary research. We should be building environments where people are better equipped to thrive. This can only be done if early support and ongoing development is prioritised, even if the process is challenging. Creating a culture of emotional intelligence needs to be an ongoing, collective effort. This will take commitment from all of us to build practical ways that help communities navigate life's emotional storms and turn setbacks into opportunities for growth, connection, and resilience.

-16-
Accountability and the Future of a Relationship

There is a moment after discharge that no one prepares you for.

The swelling has eased. The urgency has faded. The messages slow, then stop.

What remains is a quiet so dense it feels airless. In that stillness, the victim sits alone, suspended between what has happened and what comes next, in that moment, a question arises that they never imagined would be theirs to ask:

What happens now?

Introduction

While physical injuries may heal, emotional injuries, unseen and often hidden, do not follow the same process. Emotional healing has its' own rhythm, pertinent to the individual. A fracture caused by a stranger triggers' responses like anger, fear, revenge or avoidance. Yet a fracture caused by a friend elicits a much more complex array of emotions. The "victim" is often left with a gnawing mix of betrayal and confusion, as the same question circles relentlessly in their mind:

"Was it my fault?"

As the silence stretches on, grief seeps in, not just for what was lost, but for the slow, devastating realisation that the friendship may be ending, or perhaps was never real to begin with.

When harm is inflicted by a friend, someone once trusted, the road forward is neither straight nor gentle. The emotional fallout is heavy, and the legal choices are complex and overwhelming. At the end of this chapter, we offer some tools, not as easy answers but as a guide, to help navigate what is often an arduous and baffling path.

16.1 The Dynamics

When an injury is caused by a friend, possibly fuelled by frustration, a feeling of inadequacy or envy, the victim experiences two shocks simultaneously:

1. The physical injury, which demands medical treatment.

2. The relational injury, which disrupts fundamental assumptions, such as friends are not seen as a danger to one's safety.

Studies on betrayal trauma suggest that harm from a trusted person activates deeper emotional pain than harm from a stranger.

Findings from Betrayal Trauma Theory (BTT) have found that trauma from a trusted person, referred to as high betrayal, creates a more profound psychological distress, such as anxiety, Post-Traumatic Stress Disorder (PTSD) self-blame and confusion, than identical harm from a stranger because the brain struggles to reconcile contradictory truths such as,

"This person cares about me" and "This person hurt me".

This disconnect becomes the emotional anchor of the aftermath.

16.2 How Friends Become Emotional Collateral

Much of frustration-driven aggression is misdirected. The aggressor is not reacting to the "victim", they are reacting to their own failure, their own inadequacy or their own perceived humiliation. The friend becomes a "safe" outlet because the aggressor believes, consciously or not:

"They won't leave. They won't retaliate. They'll understand." But once harm is done, that assumption collapses, exposing it as both wrong and profoundly unfair.

Accountability

After a violent or reckless outburst, true accountability involves more than remorse or an apology. It requires:
- **Accurate naming of the event**, not a diminishment of its significance by labelling it an "accident," "slip," or a "misunderstanding."
- **Acknowledgment of the harm**: physical, emotional and financial.
- **Active participation in repairing the damage** by offering practical support, financial compensation and by being present.
- **Demonstrated behavioural change**, seeking anger management support and impulse control.
- **Avoidance of minimisation, denial and revisionism.** Rejecting the impulse to say, "It wasn't that bad," or to quietly rewrite the past until the memory of the incident fades.

Revisionism reshapes reality to protect the offender, not the truth, leaving the injured party unheard and the wound unhealed. Trust cannot survive without accountability and even with it, restoration of a friendship or any relationship where there has been trust, solidarity and affection, is fragile.

16.3 Ending the Friendship: Is It Justified?

Absolutely. A victim is justified in ending the friendship when:
- They no longer feel physically or emotionally safe in the company of that person.
- The friend minimises, denies or alters the event.
- The friend offers no financial, practical or emotional support.
- The wellbeing of the "victim" deteriorates in the "friend's" presence.
- Forgiveness feels forced.

No matter how long a friendship has lasted it does not outweigh the importance of recognising the right to personal safety. A historical friendship cannot cancel a moment of violent aggression that leads to severe injury, a permanent disability or worse.

Snapshot: Breaking Point

The following is an example to demonstrate the arguments above. Daniel and Mark had been friends for over twelve years, they played football together every week.

One afternoon during a game, Mark, frustrated by his repeated mistakes, shoved Daniel with disproportionate force, fracturing Daniel's knee. At the hospital, Mark insisted, *"What a shame you slipped."*

For Daniel, Mark's denial and attempt to change the story, cut deeper than the injury.

Recovery required months of physiotherapy, unpaid leave, and emotional turmoil. Mark's refusal to acknowledge what he had done left Daniel carrying the injury alone, both physically, emotionally and financially.

In the end, Daniel chose to end the friendship, not out of revenge, but to establish clarity and have some peace of mind. The trust on which the friendship had been built no longer existed.

16.4 Understanding the Psychology of the Betrayal

Victims of friend-inflicted harm often experience the following.

16.4.1 Collapse of Assumed Safety

The friend, once a source of comfort, becomes associated with unpredictability. This causes the "victim" to be constantly on guard, possibly overly vigilant which creates unnecessary stress.

16.4.2 Identity Shock

Victims ask:
- Should I have seen this coming?
- Did I provoke it?
- Why didn't they control themselves around me?

This reflects disruption of self-trust, not actual fault.

16.4.3 Relational Grief

The victim mourns not only the injury, but the loss of who they believed their friend was. Research on attachment disruptions shows this grief follows patterns like bereavement.

16.4.4 Should the Victim Consider Legal Action?

Many victims fear that reporting a friend or pursuing compensation is "too extreme."

Yet injury has consequences such as medical bills, lost earnings and long-term disability. The aggressor's emotional discomfort must not outweigh the victim's right to justice and recovery.

16.5 When May the Victim Consider Legal Action?

A victim may consider legal action when,

i)   The aggressor acted recklessly or violently.
ii)   The injury is serious, such as a fracture, ligament tear, head trauma.
iii)   The aggressor denies or minimises the event.
iv)   Financial loss makes recovery difficult.
v)   The victim fears recurrence or harm to others.

The law recognises violence even when friendship obscures its social framing.

16.6 UK Legal Options

(Below we outline some information for the readers information only, this is not legal advice)

Criminal Law

- Assault Occasioning Actual Bodily Harm (ABH)
- Grievous Bodily Harm (GBH) Section 20 or Section 18

Both may apply when injuries such as fractures or significant soft-tissue damage occur.

Civil Law

Victims may pursue compensation for:

- Medical costs
- Rehabilitation
- Loss of earnings
- Psychological injury
- Reduced quality of life

CICA (Criminal Injuries Compensation Authority)

An alternative route for financial support if the incident is reported to police and meets injury thresholds.

Restorative Justice

Available only when both parties agree and when the aggressor accepts responsibility.

16.7 Why This Matters Beyond the Individual

Understanding frustration is not just a personal insight, it has wider implications. In education, there is growing recognition that emotional regulation should be taught alongside academic skills. Equipping students with the ability to manage setbacks early can reduce the likelihood of frustration escalating into harmful behaviour later in life. In the workplace, organisations are beginning to recognise the impact of emotional pressure on performance and relationships. Environments that prioritise clear communication, realistic expectations, and supportive leadership are better equipped to reduce conflict and improve outcomes.

At a broader level, communities and institutions play a critical role. Access to mental health support, early intervention programmes, and public awareness initiatives can help identify risk factors before they escalate. The challenge is no longer understanding that frustration matters. It is acting on that understanding.

16.8 Turning Insight into Action

The research is clear: early recognition changes outcomes. When people learn to identify emotional triggers early, before reactions intensify, they are far more likely to respond with awareness rather than impulse.

This creates a crucial window for regulation, where perspective can be regained and escalation avoided.

At the same time, supportive environments play an equally important role. When systems are in place that encourage reflection, provide guidance, and reduce unnecessary pressure, the likelihood of conflict or harmful behaviour decreases significantly.

This principle applies across all levels:

- Individuals, who benefit from recognising internal signals and developing self-regulation

- Organisations, which can shape environments through leadership, communication, and realistic expectations

- Communities, where access to support, education, and early intervention can reduce wider social impact

The answer is clear, small, timely actions can prevent far more significant consequences later.

Conclusion

When harm comes from someone once trusted, the impact reaches far beyond the injury itself. The body bears the wound, but the mind is left grappling with shock, grief and the collapse of assumptions that once made the relationship feel safe.

Friendship, when fractured by violence or recklessness, becomes a source of confusion rather than comfort.

What follows is rarely straightforward. Accountability may create the conditions for repair, but it cannot promise it. Ending a relationship may be an act to protect oneself, not cruelty, revenge or rejection.

Seeking clarity through formal legal action, is not an overreaction, but a response to a reality that has already irrevocably changed.

If there is a guiding truth to hold onto, it is this: harm should not be minimised, and personal health and safety should come before loyalty. When trust is broken through violence, responsibility lies with the one who caused the harm.

When the injured party, chooses distance and boundaries, this is not abandonment, it is survival, and often the first step toward healing.

That said, this is only part of the picture.

Pressure Cooker

As this book has shown, moments like these rarely emerge in isolation. They are often the result of pressures, patterns, and missed signals that build over time.

Understanding frustration, how it develops, how it escalates, and how it can be recognised earlier, creates the opportunity to intervene before harm occurs.

The research is clear, early awareness leads to better outcomes. At every level, whether it is as an individual, an organisation, or a community, small, timely actions can prevent future consequences.

As you put this book down, here are a few thoughts to take away with you.

The way we respond to frustration is rarely random. It is shaped over time, by our early and very unique experiences, by the environments and cultures we live in, and by what we have learned to expect of ourselves and others.

Some responses are reinforced. Others can be reshaped. The more we understand what works, the more likely those changes will last.

Frustration will always be part of being human, but how we understand it, how we respond to it, and how we support each other through it, that's what determines whether it leads to harm, or growth.

REFERENCES

Adams, J.S. (1965) 'Inequity in social exchange', in Berkowitz, L. (ed.) *Advances in Experimental Social Psychology*. Vol. 2. New York: Academic Press, pp. 267–299.

Ainsworth, M.D.S., Blehar, M.C., Waters, E. and Wall, S. (1978) *Patterns of Attachment: A Psychological Study of the Strange Situation*. Hillsdale, NJ: Lawrence Erlbaum.

Anonymous (n.d.) 'I was advised to try journalling after the incident as a way to externalise the turbulent thoughts associated with post traumatic symptoms.' Unpublished online review (source details not provided).

Aronson, E. (1969) 'The theory of cognitive dissonance: A current perspective', in Berkowitz, L. (ed.) *Advances in Experimental Social Psychology*. Vol. 4. New York: Academic Press, pp. 1–34.

Beck, A.T. (1967) *Depression: Clinical, Experimental, and Theoretical Aspects*. Philadelphia, PA: University of Pennsylvania Press.

Berkowitz, L. (1989) 'Frustration-aggression hypothesis: examination and reformulation', *Psychological Bulletin*, 106(1), pp. 59–73.

Bowlby, J. (1969) *Attachment and Loss: Vol. 1. Attachment*. New York: Basic Books.

Brantley, M. and Robbins, D.D. (2022) 'The Poetry of Walker by Alice Walker', *EBSCO Research Starters*. Available at: https://www.ebsco.com/research-starters/literature-and-writing/poetry-walker-alice-walker.

Business News Week (2025) 'Loving others and being loved in return contributes to happiness'. Available at: https://businessnewsweek.in/news/loving-others-and-being-loved-in-return-contributes-to-happiness/.

Bush, R.A.B. and Folger, J.P. (2005) *The Promise of Mediation: Responding to Conflict Through Empowerment and Recognition*. San Francisco, CA: Jossey-Bass.

Carroll, R. (2005) 'Finding the words to say it: The healing power of poetry', *Evidence-Based Complementary and Alternative Medicine*, 2(2), pp. 161–172. Available at: https://pmc.ncbi.nlm.nih.gov/articles/PMC1142208/ .

Cooper, J. (2007) *Cognitive Dissonance: 50 Years of a Classic Theory*. Thousand Oaks, CA: Sage.

Cox, M.J. and Paley, B. (1997) 'Families as systems', *Annual Review of Psychology*, 48(1), pp. 243–267.

Davis, L. and Roberts, P. (2021) 'Social comparison and emotional outcomes in competitive environments', *Journal of Interpersonal Psychology*, 35(2), pp. 156–172.

De Botton, A. and The School of Life (2020) *The School of Life: An Emotional Education*. London: Penguin Books.

DePrince, A.P. (2001) 'Emotional information processing in dissociative survivors of betrayal trauma', *Journal of Trauma & Dissociation*, 2(2), pp. 9–35.

Dollard, J., Doob, L.W., Miller, N.E., Mowrer, O.H. and Sears, R.R. (1939) *Frustration and Aggression*. New Haven, CT: Yale University Press.

Downey, G. and Feldman, S.I. (1996) 'Implications of rejection sensitivity for intimate relationships', *Journal of Personality and Social Psychology*, 70(6), pp. 1327–1343.

Dweck, C.S. (2006) *Mindset: The New Psychology of Success*. New York: Random House.

Evans, R., Lee, M. and Carter, S. (2023) 'Neurochemical dysregulation and impulsive aggression: A clinical perspective', *Neuropsychology Today*, 12(1), pp. 89–104.

Festinger, L. (1954) 'A theory of social comparison processes', *Human Relations*, 7(2), pp. 117–140.

Festinger, L. (1957) *A Theory of Cognitive Dissonance*. Stanford, CA: Stanford University Press.

Field, T. (2011) 'Yoga clinical research review', *Complementary Therapies in Clinical Practice*, 17(1), pp. 1–8.

Folkman, S. and Moskowitz, J.T. (2000) 'Positive affect and the other side of coping', *American Psychologist*, 55(6), pp. 647–654.

Ford, J.D. and Gómez, J.M. (2015) 'The relationship of psychological trauma and dissociative and posttraumatic stress disorders to nonsuicidal self-injury
and suicidality: a review', *Journal of Trauma & Dissociation*, 16(3), pp. 232–271.

Freud, S. (1926) *Inhibitions, Symptoms and Anxiety*. London: International Psychoanalytic Publishing.

Freyd, J.J. (1996) *Betrayal Trauma: The Logic of Forgetting Childhood Abuse*. Cambridge, MA: Harvard University Press.

Garcia, A. and Thompson, J. (2020) 'The neural basis of emotion regulation: A review', *Brain Research Reviews*, 67(3), pp. 303–320.

Goleman, D. (1995) *Emotional Intelligence: Why It Can Matter More Than IQ*. New York: Bantam Books.

Gross, J.J. (2015) 'Emotion regulation: Current status and future prospects', *Psychological Inquiry*, 26(1), pp. 1–26.

Hannah, C. (2024) 'Trauma healing and the extraordinary hidden power of poetry', *Medium*, 21 June. Available at:
https://medium.com/@catherinehannahpoetry/trauma-healing-and-the-extraordinary-hidden-power-of-poetry-f31eeb679837.

Harris, D., Nguyen, T. and Patel, S. (2021) 'Cortisol, adrenaline, and aggression: Linking stress hormones to behavior', *Stress and Health*, 37(4), pp. 542–556.

Harter, S. (2012) *The Construction of the Self: Developmental and Sociocultural Foundations*. 2nd edn. New York: Guilford Press.

Hayes, S.C. (2004) *Acceptance and Commitment Therapy: Theory, Research, and Practice*. New York: Guilford Press.

Higgins, E.T. (1987) 'Self-discrepancy: A theory relating self and affect', *Psychological Review*, 94(3), pp. 319–340.

Hölzel, B.K., Carmody, J., Vangel, M., Congleton, C., Yerramsetti, S.M., Gard, T. and Lazar, S.W. (2011) 'Mindfulness practice leads to increases in regional brain gray matter density', *Psychiatry Research: Neuroimaging*, 191(1), pp. 36–43.

on Psychological Science, 6(6), pp. 537–559.

Hölzel, B.K., Lazar, S.W., Gard, T., Schuman-Olivier, Z., Vago, D.R. and Ott, U. (2011) 'How does mindfulness meditation work? Proposing mechanisms of action from a conceptual and neural perspective', *Perspectives*

Johnson, M. and Miller, R. (2021) 'Personality traits and frustration tolerance: A meta-analytic review', *Personality and Individual Differences*, 168, pp. 110–119.

Kabat-Zinn, J. (1994) *Wherever You Go, There You Are: Mindfulness Meditation in Everyday Life*. New York: Hyperion.

Kalter, L. (2021) 'How poetry therapy can help you tap your creative side to overcome depression, PTSD, and more', *Business Insider*, 2 March. Available at: https://www.businessinsider.com/reference/poetry-therapy.

Khoury, B., Lecomte, T., Fortin, G., Masse, M., Therien, P., Bouchard, V. and Hofmann, S.G. (2013) 'Mindfulness-based therapy: A comprehensive meta-analysis', *Clinical Psychology Review*, 33(6), pp. 763–771.

Kim, H. and Park, J. (2020) 'Attributional styles and their role in emotional responses to failure', *Cognitive Therapy and Research*, 44(6), pp. 1045–1058.

Lazar, S.W., Kerr, C.E., Wasserman, R.H., Gray, J.R., Greve, D.N., Treadway, M.T. and Fischl, B. (2005) 'Meditation experience is associated with increased cortical thickness', *Neuroreport*, 16(17), pp. 1893–1897.

Lazarus, R.S. (1991) *Emotion and Adaptation*. New York: Oxford University Press.

Lee, S., Chen, A. and Rivera, M. (2022) 'Identity, self-concept, and emotional resilience: New frontiers in psychological research', *Journal of Identity Studies*, 29(1), pp. 45–62.

Linehan, M. (2015) *DBT Skills Training Manual*. 2nd edn. New York: Guilford Press.

Martin, C.G., Cromer, L.D., DePrince, A.P. and Freyd, J.J. (2013) 'The role of cumulative trauma, betrayal, and appraisals in understanding trauma symptomatology', *Psychological Trauma: Theory, Research, Practice, and Policy*, 5(2), pp. 110–118. Available at: https://pmc.ncbi.nlm.nih.gov/articles/PMC3608140/.

Martinez, F., Liu, Y. and Thompson, D. (2023) 'Performance pressure and emotional regulation in high-stakes environments', *Performance Psychology*, 18(2), pp. 137–153.

Masten, A.S. (2001) 'Ordinary magic: Resilience processes in development', *American Psychologist*, 56(3), pp. 227–238.

Mayo Clinic (n.d.) 'Post-traumatic stress disorder (PTSD)'. Available at: https://www.mayoclinic.org/diseases-conditions/post-traumatic-stress-disorder/symptoms-causes/syc-20355967.

Mayer, J.D. and Salovey, P. (1997) 'What is emotional intelligence?', in Salovey, P. and Sluyter, D. (eds.) *Emotional Development and Emotional Intelligence: Educational Implications*. New York: Basic Books, pp. 3–31.

Mikulincer, M. and Shaver, P.R. (2007) *Attachment in Adulthood: Structure, Dynamics, and Change*. New York: Guilford Press.

Minuchin, S. (1974) *Families and Family Therapy*. Cambridge, MA: Harvard University Press.

National Health Service (NHS) (n.d.) 'Post-traumatic stress disorder (PTSD): Overview'. Available at: https://www.nhs.uk/mental-health/conditions/post-traumatic-stress-disorder-ptsd/overview/.

National Institute of Mental Health (n.d.) 'Post-traumatic stress disorder (PTSD)'. Available at: https://www.nimh.nih.gov/health/publications/post-traumatic-stress-disorder-ptsd.

Neff, K.D. (2003) 'The development and validation of a scale to measure self-compassion', *Self and Identity*, 2(3), pp. 223–250.

Nguyen, L., Garcia, E. and Wong, P. (2022) 'Cognitive appraisal and emotional reactivity in stressful situations', *Journal of Cognitive Neuroscience*, 34(5), pp. 783–799.

Nolen-Hoeksema, S., Wisco, B.E. and Lyubomirsky, S. (2008) 'Rethinking rumination', *Perspectives on Psychological Science*, 3(5), pp. 400–424.

Perloff, R.M. (2014) 'Social media effects on young women's body image concerns: Theoretical perspectives and an agenda for research', *Sex Roles*, 71(11–12), pp. 363–377.

Roberts, K. and Allen, J. (2023) 'Expectancy violation and the dynamics of frustration: Implications for educational settings', *Educational Psychology Review*, 35(1), pp. 95–113.

Rosenberg, M. (1965) *Society and the Adolescent Self-Image*. Princeton, NJ: Princeton University Press.

Sapolsky, R.M. (1998) *Why Zebras Don't Get Ulcers: An Updated Guide to Stress, Stress-Related Diseases, and Coping*. New York: W. H. Freeman.

Segal, Z.V., Williams, J.M.G. and Teasdale, J.D. (2013) *Mindfulness-Based Cognitive Therapy for Depression*. New York: Guilford Press.

Smith, J., Patel, R. and Brown, C. (2023) 'Emotional triggers in the modern world: A comprehensive analysis', *Contemporary Psychology*, 41(3), pp. 201–218.

Steele, C.M. (1988) 'The psychology of self-affirmation: Sustaining the integrity of the self', in Berkowitz, L. (ed.) *Advances in Experimental Social Psychology*. Vol. 21. New York: Academic Press, pp. 261–302.

Tangney, J.P., Stuewig, J. and Mashek, D.J. (2007) 'Moral emotions and moral behaviour', *Annual Review of Psychology*, 58, pp. 345–372.

Valkenburg, P.M., Peter, J. and Schouten, A.P. (2006) 'Friend networking sites and their relationship to adolescents' well-being and social self-esteem', *CyberPsychology & Behavior*, 9(5), pp. 584–590.

Van Veen, V., Krug, M.K., Schooler, J.W. and Carter, C.S. (2009) 'Neural activity predicts attitude change in cognitive dissonance', *Nature Neuroscience*, 12(11), pp. 1469–1474.

Walker, L.E.A. (2017) *The Battered Woman Syndrome*. 5th edn. New York: Springer.

THE GLOSSARY

Achievement-Contingent Self-Esteem Framework

A model proposing that an individual's self-worth is dependent on achievement outcomes, causing self-esteem to fluctuate with success and failure.

Actual Self

The attributes and qualities a person believes they currently possess.

Adrenal Cortex

The outer layer of the adrenal glands responsible for producing cortisol and other glucocorticoids.

Adrenocorticotropic Hormone (ACTH)

A hormone released by the pituitary gland that stimulates the adrenal cortex to produce cortisol.

Allostatic Overload

The cumulative physiological strain placed on the body through repeated or chronic stress activation.

Amygdala

A brain structure central to emotional processing, particularly fear and threat detection.

Anterior Cingulate Cortex (ACC)

A region of the brain involved in emotional regulation, conflict monitoring, and error detection.

Antipathetic

Displaying dislike, opposition, or hostility.

Attribution Theory

A psychological theory examining how individuals interpret and explain the causes of events and behaviours.

Attributional Style

A person's habitual way of explaining success and failure, often along dimensions such as internal/external or stable/unstable causes.

Atherosclerosis

The narrowing and hardening of arteries due to plaque buildup, increasing cardiovascular risk

Arrhythmias

Irregular heart rhythms that may result from physiological stress or systemic dysfunction.

Cardiovascular Impact

The effects of psychological or physiological stress on heart and vascular functioning.

Catecholamines

Stress-related hormones, including epinephrine and norepinephrine, released during sympathetic nervous system activation.

Cognitive Defusion

A psychological technique involving distancing oneself from thoughts rather than becoming entangled in them.

Cognitive Dissonance

Psychological discomfort arising from holding conflicting beliefs, values, or behaviours.

Cognitive Neoassociation Theory.

Leonard Berkowitz fundamentally reshaped how psychologists understand the link between frustration and aggression. The original 1939 model from John Dollard and colleagues argued that frustration automatically leads to aggression. Berkowitz believed that was too rigid and too simple. Instead, he proposed what became known as Cognitive Neoassociation Theory.

At the heart of Berkowitz's theory is one key shift: Frustration does not directly cause aggression. It first produces negative affect, particularly anger. That emotional state then activates related thoughts, memories, and action tendencies in the brain. These associations are linked like a network. When anger is triggered, aggressive ideas and impulses become more accessible. Think of it like flipping a switch in the mind. Frustration creates an unpleasant emotional charge.

That charge activates connected mental pathways, hostile thoughts, aggressive scripts, past memories of conflict. Whether aggression actually happens depends on what else is present in the environment and how the situation is interpreted. One of Berkowitz's most famous contributions is the "weapons effect." In experiments, participants who were angered behaved more aggressively when weapons were present in the room compared to neutral objects. The weapons acted as aggressive cues, activating aggressive associations already primed by anger. In other words, frustration loads the emotional system, and environmental cues help determine whether it fires.

Importantly, Berkowitz emphasised that aggression is more likely when:
- The frustration feels unjust or intentional
- The person interprets the situation as hostile
- Aggressive cues are present
- The individual lacks strong inhibitory controls

But aggression is not inevitable. Cognitive appraisal, how we interpret what happened, can dampen or escalate the response. If a blocked goal is seen as accidental or unavoidable, anger may be weaker. If it is seen as deliberate or unfair, aggression becomes more likely. To conclude, in Berkowitz's model, frustration becomes a trigger for anger, anger activates aggressive networks, and context determines whether those impulses turn into action. It's a far more nuanced and psychologically realistic account than the original "frustration equals aggression" formula.

Cortisol

A glucocorticoid hormone released during stress that influences metabolism, immune response, and energy regulation.

Displacement

A defence mechanism in which emotional reactions are redirected from their original source to a safer substitute target.

Dysphoric

A general state of emotional unease, dissatisfaction, or discomfort.

Endocrine Balance

The stable and regulated functioning of the body's hormonal systems.

Epinephrine

Also known as adrenaline; a hormone central to the fight-or-flight response.

Fixed Mindset

The belief that intelligence or ability is innate and unchangeable.

Glucocorticoids

A class of steroid hormones, including cortisol, involved in stress regulation and metabolism.

Growth Mindset

The belief that ability and intelligence can develop through effort, strategy, and learning.

Hippocampus

A brain region involved in memory formation and regulation of stress responses.

Hippocampal Neurogenesis

The formation of new neurons in the hippocampus, which may be reduced under chronic stress.

HPA Axis (Hypothalamic–Pituitary–Adrenal Axis)

This is the body's central stress-response system, linking the brain and endocrine system to regulate how we react to stress. When the brain perceives a threat or pressure, the hypothalamus releases **corticotropin-releasing hormone (CRH)**, which signals the pituitary gland to release **adrenocorticotropic hormone (ACTH)**. ACTH then travels through the bloodstream to the adrenal glands, triggering the release of **cortisol**, the body's primary stress hormone.

Cortisol prepares the body to deal with the challenge by increasing energy availability, sharpening attention, mobilizing glucose, and temporarily suppressing non-essential processes such as digestion. Once enough cortisol has been released, it sends feedback signals to the brain that reduce further hormone production, helping the body return to balance.

In performers and athletes, the HPA axis is frequently activated during competitions, public evaluation, high-pressure performances, or fear of making mistakes. Short bursts of this response can enhance focus and energy, but when stress becomes chronic the system can remain overactivated, leading to fatigue, anxiety, impaired concentration, and ultimately **allostatic overload**, the cumulative physiological strain caused by prolonged stress.

Ideal Self
The version of oneself that represents aspirations, goals, or desired qualities.

Internalisation
The process by which external values, expectations, or beliefs become integrated into one's own identity and self-concept.

Longitudinal Studies
Research designs that follow the same individuals over extended periods to observe changes over time.

Maladaptive
Patterns of thinking or behaviour that are ineffective, harmful, or counterproductive.

Metabolic Disturbances
Disruptions in metabolic functioning, often associated with chronic stress.

Negative Self-Schemas
Deeply held, often critical beliefs about oneself that shape perception and reinforce low self-worth.

Neurotransmitter

A chemical messenger that transmits signals between neurons in the brain.

Ought Self

The version of oneself shaped by perceived obligations, duties, and external expectations.

Performance Pressure

Stress arising from perceived expectations to achieve or perform at a high level.

Perfectionism

The tendency to set excessively high standards and base self-worth on flawless performance.

Prefrontal Cortex (PFC)

A brain region responsible for executive functioning, decision-making, and emotional regulation.

Psychological Crucible

An intense emotional or psychological experience that produces significant personal transformation.

SAM Activation (Sympathetic–Adrenal–Medullary Activation)

A rapid stress-response system involving the release of catecholamines.

It works in parallel with the HPA axis, the SAM axis governs the immediate, rapid responses to stress.

Activation of this axis leads to the release of catecholamines, namely adrenaline (epinephrine) and noradrenaline (norepinephrine), from the adrenal medulla. These neurotransmitters prepare the body for rapid action by increasing heart rate, elevating blood pressure, and diverting blood flow to skeletal muscles.

While the SAM system is critical for short-term survival, its chronic activation, as seen in emotional overload, can lead to cardiovascular strain, arrhythmias, and metabolic disturbances.

The interplay between the HPA and SAM axes creates a complex neurochemical milieu that can both support acute functioning and when overtaxed, precipitate systemic dysfunction.

Self-Concept

The broad, holistic understanding of one's identity, including beliefs, self-image, and self-esteem.

Self-Image

The mental representation of one's physical appearance and observable traits.

Self-Integrity

The perception of oneself as morally adequate, competent, and worthy.

Self-Justification

Cognitive processes used to defend or rationalise actions in order to reduce psychological discomfort.

Self-Schemas

Cognitive frameworks that organise beliefs and knowledge about oneself.

Serotonin

A neurotransmitter involved in mood regulation, sleep, and emotional balance.

Systemic Dysfunction

Widespread disruption across interconnected bodily systems.

The Frustration-Aggression Hypothesis

This theory was first laid out in 1939 by a group of Yale psychologists: John Dollard, Neal E. Miller, Leonard W. Doob, O. H. Mowrer, and Robert R. Sears and boils down to a simple, very human idea: when something blocks you from getting what you want, you get frustrated. Their original claim was strong and direct: frustration always leads to some form of aggression, and aggression always comes from frustration. In their view, the emotional pressure builds, and aggression is the natural release valve. Neal E. Miller softened the original hypothesis by reframing frustration as creating an aggressive drive rather than guaranteeing aggression. Albert Bandura, whose social learning theory showed that whether someone "fights back" depends heavily on what they've learned about aggression being rewarded or punished. John W. Burton, in conflict theory, framed unmet human needs as forces that drive confrontational or corrective action, which is closer to the idea of frustration becoming an externalised push for redress.

Type 2 Diabetes

A metabolic disorder involving insulin resistance, sometimes associated with chronic stress and visceral fat accumulation.

Visceral Fat

Fat stored around internal organs, associated with metabolic and cardiovascular risk.

Whitewash

To minimise, conceal, or make wrongdoing appear less serious than it is.

A Compelling Voice on the Dynamics of Human Behaviour

Closing Reflection

Permission to be Ridiculous.

Laughter may be one of the most civilised ways we release pressure. In a life shaped by expectation, comparison, and quiet frustration, a wobble every now and then is inevitable, that awkward pause, that gaffe at a work dinner or the carefully constructed plan that collapses.

We don't laugh at perfection. We laugh at the crack in it.

Our intention is not to be cruel, but we recognise our own fallibility in someone else's stumble. It is in that moment we see our own shortcomings, our own carefully managed façade that, just for a moment, we let slip.

Frustration thrives in secrecy, convincing us that our struggles are private failures. Humour disrupts that lie. It exposes the shared absurdity of trying to appear endlessly composed in a world that constantly tests us.

It transforms private shame into shared humanity and in that brief moment of collective laughter, the pressure cooker does not explode, but hisses, releasing our pent-up tension.

Laughter does not trivialise difficulty. It humanises it. It reminds us that imperfection is not a personal failure but a universal condition.

Perhaps that is what gives us relief: we were never meant to be flawless, only alive, adjusting, and occasionally wobbling with the rest of humanity.

We are human, always glorious and occasionally imperfect.

THE END